Philosophy Smackdown

T0056402

To Theo and Lola

Philosophy Smackdown

Douglas Edwards

polity

First published in 2020 by Polity Press

Polity Press
65 Bridge Street
Cambridge CB2 1UR, UK

Polity Press
101 Station Landing
Suite 300
Medford, MA 02155, USA

ISBN-13: 978-1-5095-3765-5
ISBN-13: 978-1-5095-3766-2(pb)

A catalogue record for this book is available from the British Library.

Library of Congress Cataloging-in-Publication Data

Names: Edwards, Douglas, 1958- author. | Polity Press.
Title: Philosophy smackdown / Douglas Edwards.
Description: Medford, Massachusetts : Polity, 2020. | Summary: "Hulk Hogan and Socrates wrestle with the big ideas"-- Provided by publisher.
Identifiers: LCCN 2019038633 (print) | LCCN 2019038634 (ebook) | ISBN 9781509537655 (Hardback) | ISBN 9781509537662 (Paperback) | ISBN 9781509537679 (ePUB)
Subjects: LCSH: Wrestling. | Sports--Philosophy.
Classification: LCC GV1195 .E39 2020 (print) | LCC GV1195 (ebook) | DDC 796.812--dc23
LC record available at https://lccn.loc.gov/2019038633
LC ebook record available at https://lccn.loc.gov/2019038634

Typeset in 10/16.5pt Charter ITC by
Servis Filmsetting Ltd, Stockport, Cheshire
Printed and bound in Great Britain by CPI Group (UK) Ltd, Croydon

For further information on Polity, visit our website: politybooks.com

Table of Contests

Preshow

1. Origins

For me, it started with videotapes when I was about 10 or 11 years old. My younger brother Glyn would borrow them from his friend, and we would watch enraptured as these giant characters in colorful costumes grappled and slammed each other in the ring. Mostly World Wrestling Federation (WWF) WrestleManias, we watched Hogan beat Savage, Warrior beat Hogan, and then Warrior return to save Hogan. Growing up in the south of England, we had little idea where this was happening (apart from that it was in America), but we watched as much as we could. Action figures and posters followed – I remember marveling at my friend Justin's Legion of Doom poster, with Hawk and Animal snarling in their face paint and spiked football shoulder pads.

The moment when I really became gripped, though, was WrestleMania X, and the triumph of Bret "Hitman" Hart. Bret, at the time a classic babyface, or good guy, was a spirited, plucky hero in distinctive pink and black attire, who, despite not being the biggest guy in comparison to behemoths like Hulk and Warrior, relied on his technical expertise and skill to work his way to the top. At the time Bret was feuding with his brother Owen, and the story of their feud resonated with me. A classic story of sibling rivalry, it hit close to home: my brother and I constantly competed and strove to beat each other, no matter what we were doing. Only 18 months apart, we played pretty much any game you could think of, and the story was always the same. Me, trying to prove that, because I was older, I was better, and him trying to show that that was nonsense. Bret and Owen's feud, pitched as it was with Bret the babyface and Owen the heel (bad guy) spoke to my 11-year-old self as a mirror of my experience: Bret even had brown hair, and Owen blonde hair, just like me and my brother!

After a shock loss to Owen in the opening match of WrestleMania X (which is also regarded as one of the best matches of all time), Bret overcame the odds to defeat the huge Yokozuna in the main event to become the WWF Champion. All the other good guys came out from the back to celebrate, lifting him up on their shoulders, as Owen looked on, scowling.

This cemented Bret's status as my hero. And my brother, obviously, mocked me mercilessly for this whenever the opportunity arose. He would support whoever Bret faced. When I bought a Bret action figure, he bought a Ric Flair one. When we would wrestle at home, he would always assume the character of whoever Bret was facing at the time, while I valiantly tried to work out how to lock him in the Sharpshooter, Bret's finishing submission hold. I think I only managed it once, but it was great. He got his revenge with a Pedigree on a block of wood.

As we progressed through our teens, we were lucky to get Sky TV at home, which meant we could watch WWF weekly shows and monthly pay per views. In 1997 – a pivotal year for the WWF – we watched Bret's feud with Stone Cold Steve Austin, culminating in the spectacular submission match at WrestleMania 13. 1997 saw Bret become WWF Champion again, and progressed ominously towards his showdown with long-term nemesis Shawn Michaels at Survivor Series. After a long brawl, the match was reaching its culmination when Michaels put Hart in Hart's own sharpshooter move. In a confusing sequence, the referee called for the bell, and Hart looked bewildered as Michaels went to the back celebrating. "Haha, he submitted", crowed my brother, as I looked at the screen fading to black in disbelief – no, he *can't* have done, he's Bret Hart! What just happened?

We didn't know it at the time, but we had just witnessed one of the most seismic and controversial moments in pro wrestling history, and one that would change the pro wrestling industry: the Montreal Screwjob. It was an event that would open the doors to the "reality" behind the wrestling business, and be of great interest to me later on, as a philosopher.

Soon after this, my brother lost interest in wrestling, and I started watching it with my friend Chris. We were watching during the legendary "Attitude Era" of the late 1990s/early 2000s, when Stone Cold Steve Austin and The Rock reigned supreme. We would stay up late into the night playing WWF No Mercy on the N64, and watch the monthly pay per views which, due to the time difference, ran from 1 a.m. to 4 a.m. on a Sunday night. We'd emerge bleary-eyed to school the next day, much to our parents' dismay. We discovered the alternatives to the WWF. WCW had the New World Order, spectacular cruiserweights like Rey Mysterio Jr. and Eddie Guerrero, and the hilarious hijinks of Chris Jericho. In the early days of online video, we'd find clips from the rebel outfit ECW of Rob Van Dam, Taz, Sabu, Rhino and the gang putting each other through tables, jumping off balconies, and kicking chairs into each other's faces. What we couldn't watch, we'd find out about through wrestling news websites, like Jimmy Van's knowyournews.com.

After Chris and I went our separate ways to university, the WWF subsumed these other companies, transformed into World Wrestling Entertainment (WWE), and I didn't watch much wrestling for a while.

During this time, I discovered philosophy, which became something of an obsession of its own, and much of my time was devoted to it through undergraduate and graduate studies, and into my academic career, the early stages of which I spent in Ireland and Scotland. I would occasionally dabble in some wrestling-related stuff on the internet (particularly CM Punk's "pipebomb" promo of 2011), but a lot of it passed me by. I did consider using the different ways you can win a wrestling match as an analogy for a view about truth I was developing, but ultimately decided against it.

Then, in 2014, I moved to the United States, and got cable TV. WWE Raw and SmackDown! were now available for me to watch live. I started watching again. I got a trial for the WWE Network and discovered all my old favorite WWF, WCW, and ECW shows from growing up. I began to learn about New Japan Pro Wrestling. I also, and this was a crucial part of my revived interest in wrestling, started listening to a number of podcasts. Starting with podcasts by former or current wrestlers Steve Austin and Chris Jericho, I went on to more fan-based productions, like *The Lawcast*, which reviewed old wrestling shows. I then branched out into the Conrad Thompson productions *Something to Wrestle with Bruce Prichard*, and *83 Weeks with Eric Bischoff*, along with contemporary review shows like *We Enjoy Wrestling* and *WrestleTalk's WrestleRamble*. Listening to these shows, and realizing the thirst for the reality behind the wrestling business that they aimed to quench, made me see pro wrestling in a whole new light.

Moreover, I started watching live wrestling, which allowed me to experience the phenomenon in a whole new way. My first live wrestling event was a WWE house show of around 3,000 fans in Utica, NY, in 2016, and since then I have attended a variety of wrestling shows, from the smallest to the largest. I have seen local promotions Dynasty Pro Wrestling and New York Championship Wrestling present shows in a local sports center in Whitesboro, NY, with around 150 fans, to a larger independent company, Northeast Wrestling, putting on shows for around 3,000 fans in Poughkeepsie, NY. I also went, with my friend Chris, to Madison Square Garden to see the New Japan Pro Wrestling/Ring of Honor G1 Supercard, with around 20,000 fans, and, the same weekend, we went to WrestleMania 35 at MetLife Stadium in New Jersey, with around 80,000 fans.

As my relationship with pro wrestling was revitalized, my career as both a teacher and writer of philosophy continued to develop, and I published a number of articles and books. After sneaking a Stone Cold Steve Austin reference into my book on truth, I began to realize that these two interests – philosophy and pro wrestling – were things that had a lot more in common than I first realized. Both are often misunderstood and marginalized in popular culture, yet seem to maintain an omnipresence on the fringes of public consciousness. Both are seen as niche activities that have little to do with the "real world". Both involve a degree of creativity and pretense, and both require flair and charisma to be done successfully (at least in terms of *teaching* philosophy!). Both prompt us to think about key questions of human life. And yet, they also seemed so different. One is cerebral, the other is physical. One is concerned with uncovering how things really are, and the other is concerned with hiding how things really are. Philosophy is supposed to be a serious intellectual pursuit for grown-ups, and pro wrestling is often seen as a silly distraction for kids.

I realized that there's a lot to explore here, and that thinking about pro wrestling from a philosophical point of view would be a fun and interesting thing to do. I looked around and saw, though, that little to no philosophical work on pro wrestling had ever been done. I said my prayers, took my vitamins, drank my milk, and got to work on this book.

2. Rundown

Welcome to *Philosophy Smackdown!* This is a book about pro wrestling and philosophy – the first of its kind. It aims to examine pro wrestling from a philosophical point of view in a way that is interesting and fun. I hope you'll agree that pro wrestling is not only one of the most impressive and unique forms of entertainment around, but also that it can prompt us to think about some deep issues concerning who we are as human beings, and how we ought to relate to each other both individually and culturally.

This is why I think pro wrestling is so apt for philosophical investigation: philosophy asks questions such as "What's reality really like beneath the appearances?", "What is it to be free?", "What makes us the people we are?", and "What is it to be a good person?", which are all questions that arise when thinking about pro wrestling. Whether it's thinking about the matches, the characters, the storylines, or the backstage politics, these questions are never far away. Pro wrestling's stubborn resistance to classification into the categories of "sport" and "art" also poses a philosophical challenge, as philosophers love giving clear definitions!

Each chapter takes a key philosophical concept and analyses its role and significance in pro wrestling. We talk through reality, freedom, identity, morality, justice, and meaning, which – I suggest – all have central roles in what pro wrestling is as a phenomenon. We work through key examples in pro wrestling history to develop the central ideas, and also reflect on how the way these issues play out in pro wrestling is mirrored in the way they play out in our "real lives". As a bonus "dark match", we also discuss the relationship between pro wrestling and philosophy itself.

Here's a brief summary of each chapter:

In *Reality*: Work vs Shoot, we explore the long-awaited encounter between what is real and what is fake. We will get to the heart of what reality is, and how pro wrestling helps us to understand the key distinction between appearance and reality. We will witness the times when that distinction breaks down in pro wrestling, known as "shoots", including the infamous "Montreal Screwjob", and discuss what being a pro wrestling fan can tell us about being responsible citizens in a democracy.

In *Freedom*: Scripting vs Spontaneity, we look at the idea that pro wrestling is scripted, and the extent to which this is a distinctive mark of pro wrestling over other sports, and real life. We explore the different extents to which pro wrestling is scripted, and discuss philosophical accounts of how "real life" is scripted. We also talk about breaking cultural scripts, look at the development of women's wrestling, and examine the controversial issue of intergender wrestling.

Identity: Person vs Gimmick delves into the relationship between a wrestler and their character, or "gimmick". We explore questions of personal identity, such as what happens to a character when the person playing them changes, and how we can make sense – if at all – of a character changing over time. We also talk about what happens when wrestlers "work themselves into a shoot", and inadvertently become their characters. We also see that the predicament of wrestlers and their gimmicks is not a million miles removed from the issues of identity we face in our everyday lives.

In *Morality*: Babyface vs Heel, we examine the age-old question of what makes a good person, and how this idea plays out in pro wrestling storylines. Of particular interest is the classic babyface/heel dynamic, and how this has evolved in the last 30 years or so. We track this using Aristotle's account of the virtues to explore how the roles of good guys and bad guys have changed, and what this tells us about our cultural interpretations of what it is to be a good person, and the aims we set for ourselves.

Justice: Prejudice vs Progress scrutinizes pro wrestling's sometimes uncomfortable relationship with issues of social justice, such as racism and homophobia. We explore some controversial cases of race and jingoism in pro wrestling storylines, and contrast different ways of approaching LGBTQ issues. We also look at what it would take for a pro wrestling company to be socially responsible, and discuss the challenges awaiting the different approaches to doing so.

In *Meaning*: Sport vs Monster, we tackle the question of what pro wrestling fundamentally is. Is it a sport? Sports entertainment? Or a "monster": something entirely resistant to categorization? We see that the issue of whether or not it is a sport is far more complex than it might seem, particularly when we clarify what sports pro wrestling is most similar to. We also trace the carnival origins of pro wrestling to develop the idea that pro wrestling is, and ought to be, in a class of its own.

The *Dark Match*: Pro Wrestling vs Philosophy offers some reflections on the similarities and differences between pro wrestling and philosophy, both as a subject, and as a discipline. It gives an insight into philosophical practice and method, and how both bear a striking resemblance to aspects of pro wrestling, such as the similarities between the narrative structures of philosophical works and pro wrestling matches, and the need for a philosopher to develop their own gimmick in order to succeed.

Pro wrestling showcases the work of some of the best athletes and entertainers that the world has ever seen. It is not often given its due as a cultural phenomenon from which we can learn much about ourselves and the world we live in, and my hope is that this book is a small step in changing that narrative. Pro wrestling's not perfect, for sure, and there are some very troubling aspects in its history – and its present – that we will reflect on seriously and critically. I hope the overwhelming feeling though on reading this is positivity and optimism for what pro wrestling can do for us.

The speed at which pro wrestling moves provides a challenge for anyone writing a book about it. I have aimed to use examples that are reasonably timeless, but note that, particularly in the sections about the social and cultural aspects of pro wrestling, things can change over time. If progress has been made in regard to some of the social issues in pro wrestling raised in this book by the time you are reading it, then that's wonderful, and I hope won't detract from your enjoyment of it.

Also, just to clarify, I'm a philosopher who's a wrestling fan, and that's the perspective from which this book is written. I don't pretend to be a wrestling journalist, or someone with expertise working in the pro wrestling business, and I hope that comes across in the text. As a philosopher, I expect many of the points made here to be conversation starters, as opposed to definitive claims. If you disagree with some of the things said, that's great – let's talk about it!

3. Thanks

I am very grateful to Pascal Porcheron at Polity for the discussions that prompted this book, and for his feedback, comments, and encouragement throughout. I'd also like to thank Ellen MacDonald-Kramer for her help and efficiency, along with a number of anonymous readers for Polity who gave very helpful comments on the proposal and the first draft of the book. I'd also like to thank Ian Tuttle for copy-editing the text.

Thanks to my colleagues in the Philosophy Department at Utica College, Chris Riddle, Leonore Fleming, and John Lawless, who have been interested in the project from the beginning, and very supportive throughout. I'm also grateful to Utica College for a grant to support a research trip for the book. Thanks too to Lisa Jones for reading the first draft of the manuscript, and to Jesse Weiner for many helpful conversations and jaunts to watch local wrestling in upstate NY.

I'd like to thank Chris Underwood, for years of fun watching and talking about wrestling together, and also for discussing the project with me many times, and reading and commenting on drafts. Thanks also to my brother, Glyn Edwards, for starting the wrestling journey with me when we were kids, and to whichever of his friends it was that lent him all those videotapes. Thanks also to my parents for getting Sky TV, and for tolerating all the wrestling madness.

I am very grateful to my wife, Alex Plakias, for encouraging me to pursue this project, for reading and commenting on drafts, and for putting up with all my wrestling podcasts, TV shows, and trips to live events. Thanks to my son Theo; it was on long walks trying to get him to sleep as a baby when I really got into wrestling podcasts. I'm surprised his first word wasn't "kayfabe" given the number of podcasts he's subsequently listened to in the car. A pre-emptive thanks too to my daughter Lola, who is blissfully unaware of all this.

I am very thankful for the number of entertaining and informative podcasts, websites, books, and documentaries on pro wrestling, which make it so much fun to be a wrestling fan. Of particular use were *The Steve Austin Show*, *Talk is Jericho*, *The Lawcast*, *We Enjoy Wrestling*, *Something to Wrestle with Bruce Prichard*, *83 Weeks with Eric Bischoff*, and *WrestleTalk's WrestleRamble*.

Last but not least, thanks to those who give us pro wrestling: the performers and promoters. I'd particularly like to thank every wrestler who has laced up a pair of boots and entered the squared circle. I hope the book conveys not only the passion I have for pro wrestling, but also my deep respect and admiration for pro wrestlers themselves. Thank you for the risks you take, the sacrifices you have made, and the pain you have endured to make such a wonderful thing possible.

4. Glossary

I'm assuming that, if you have picked up this book, you have some interest in pro wrestling, and may well know that pro wrestling has its own terminology of sorts. This is explained at relevant points in the book, but I thought it'd be handy to include a glossary of some of the key terms used here for reference.

Work:	Something that is scripted or planned.
Shoot:	When a wrestler does something that is not part of the script.
Worked-Shoot:	A pre-planned event that is made to look like it wasn't pre-planned.
Workers:	Wrestlers.
Doing the Job:	Losing a match.
Jobber:	A wrestler who loses most of their matches.
Card:	Lineup for the show.
Dark Match:	A bonus match for the live crowd that is not televised, usually at the beginning or end of the show.
The Business:	The pro wrestling business.
Heat:	(a) the response a heel wants from the crowd; or

	(b) beef between wrestlers backstage, e.g. "Bret and Shawn had heat".
Promo:	A spoken vignette on screen or in the ring, usually designed to further a feud or promote a match.
Getting Over:	What a wrestler aims to do: getting the desired crowd response (cheers for a babyface, boos for a heel).
Being Over/Over:	Getting the desired crowd response (cheers for a babyface, boos for a heel).
Going Over:	Winning a match.
Put Over:	Giving your opponent the victory. For example, "Van Dam was asked to put over Triple H".
Gimmick:	Character.
Heel:	Baddie, or villain, who the crowd is supposed to boo.
Babyface/Face:	Goodie, or hero, who the crowd is supposed to cheer.
Kayfabe:	The world as it is presented on screen and in the ring. For example, "in kayfabe, the Undertaker and Kane are brothers".
Mark:	A fan who is not "smartened up" to how pro wrestling works.
Smart fan:	A fan who is "smartened up" to how pro wrestling works, and is usually interested in the work behind the scenes.
Smart Mark/ Smark:	A smart fan who nevertheless is able to lose themselves in the show and "mark out" for key moments as if they believed it was real.
Pop:	A loud, positive, crowd reaction.

Selling: Making your opponent's moves look good by convincing the audience that they hurt.

Bury: Make someone look bad, to the point where their image looks unrecoverable.

WWF: World Wrestling Federation

WWE: World Wrestling Entertainment (in 2002, the World Wrestling Federation changed its name to World Wrestling Entertainment. In this book I use "WWF" to refer to the company pre-2002 name change, and "WWE" to refer to the company post-2002 name change)

WCW: World Championship Wrestling

ECW: Extreme Championship Wrestling

NJPW: New Japan Pro Wrestling

AEW: All Elite Wrestling

OK, enough stalling, let's get it on – RING THE BELL!

1

Reality: Work vs Shoot

The distinction between appearance and reality is something you learn early on as a pro wrestling fan. As a kid, you *believe* it's real: you believe that they are really fighting, really competing to win the match. You talk with your friends about who can beat up who, and point to wrestling matches as evidence – "of course Warrior can beat up Hogan, didn't you see WrestleMania VI?". Then, gradually, you start to question things. Older kids tell you that it's "fake". You watch the matches more carefully, and start to wonder how it is that the wrestlers pull off all these feats of strength and athleticism. In cage matches you start to wonder why they don't climb that little bit faster, or run out the door with a little more commitment.

When I was a kid there wasn't the wealth of information about the workings of pro wrestling that we have now. There were no documentaries telling all (let alone podcasts), no extensive internet discussions, and no social media accounts which told the wrestlers' real life stories, and how they differed from their in-ring lives. The discovery of the reality behind wrestling was a gradual process, that came in dribs and drabs.

One might think that finding out what's really going on would dampen one's enthusiasm for pro wrestling, but what I found instead though was that the more I saw through the appearances, the more interesting it became. This aspect of pro wrestling plays a large role in explaining the fanaticism associated with it, and in this chapter we'll be exploring this fascinating aspect of pro wrestling fandom, and what it can tell us about reality, and ourselves.

1. Three Layers of Reality in Pro Wrestling

When watching an *amateur* wrestling match, one sees two athletes competing for physical supremacy. They do so by performing various holds and throws, and obey a set of rules that govern the activity. The aim is to pin your opponent's shoulders to the mat for a short time (around a second). A referee checks that the rules are being followed, and declares a winner after a pinfall has been counted.

When watching a *pro* wrestling match, the same sort of thing seems to be going on. Wrestlers grapple each other and use throws and slams to get their opponent down to the mat, ultimately aiming to pin them. The main differences on the face of it are that pro wrestling matches can involve more than two wrestlers; that pinfalls are counts to three seconds, as opposed to one; and that you can also win by submission. Aside from that, similar holds and throws are used, a set of rules is there to be followed, and a referee is there to check that they are enforced, and to raise the hand of the winner.

Looking closely, though, we see that things are not quite as they seem. The moves tend to be a lot more acrobatic than the moves in amateur wrestling. Some moves seem impossible to pull off, and perhaps are, unless there is some cooperation involved. The wrestlers tend also to be a lot more flamboyant both in dress and demeanor. They interact with each other, and the crowd, in ways one does not find amateur wrestlers acting. They have characters, stories behind those characters, feuds with specific opponents who often interfere in their matches, and referees often are attacked or injured inadvertently. To put it in a word, there is a lot more *pageantry* than one finds in amateur wrestling.

The reason for this, of course, is that pro wrestling is not to amateur wrestling what professional soccer is to amateur soccer, i.e. a more regulated and intense version of the same activity; rather, it is a totally different beast. In pro wrestling matches, the wrestlers work together to put on a match, as opposed to work against each other to try to win the match. Indeed, rather than try to *beat* their opponent, a good pro wrestler aims to make their opponent look as good as possible. Instead of the match being a genuine contest between two athletes, it is a story told by two athletes, who cooperate, either beforehand, on the fly during the match, or both. The story told is determined by the writers, bookers, or promoters who run the shows, and dictate the characters of the wrestlers involved. The intention is to captivate the audience, thrill them with the athletic display of the match, and draw them in emotionally with the story told by the characters involved.

One key difference between amateur and pro wrestling, then, is that there is a distinction between appearance and reality in pro wrestling that there isn't in amateur wrestling. What *appears* to be a contest, is in *reality* a performance. It is this distinction that we'll focus on here.

Before we do, let's talk briefly about the f-word: isn't pro wrestling "fake", whereas amateur wrestling is "real"? There's a reason many wrestling fans refer to "fake" as the "f-word", and it's not just because it begins with "f". It's also because it's taboo. It betrays a fundamental misunderstanding of what pro wrestling is, and why people appreciate it. Now, there's no doubt that what you see in the ring is not quite "real", in the sense that the performers are putting on a *show*, which they jointly present, as opposed to being engaged in genuine competition to win the match. But to say that it's fake is to mischaracterize the activity in a way that unnecessarily denigrates the performers and the complexity of the activity. Would we call movies "fake", and actors in movies "fakers"? If not, then we shouldn't call pro wrestling "fake", or pro wrestlers "fakers" (more on this later). Instead, we should think about pro wrestling in terms of the distinction between appearance and reality, which allows us to get to the interesting issues in a more direct and accurate way.

Borrowing some ideas from the Ancient Greek philosopher Plato, let's develop this by looking at three layers of reality in pro wrestling: *appearance, reality behind the appearance,* and *true reality*, which will also help us to understand the different ways that fans engage with it. These three layers are illustrated in Plato's "Allegory of the Cave", from his work *The Republic* (see figure 1).

Plato imagines some prisoners trapped in an underground cave, tied down so they are forced to look only in one direction. Shadows

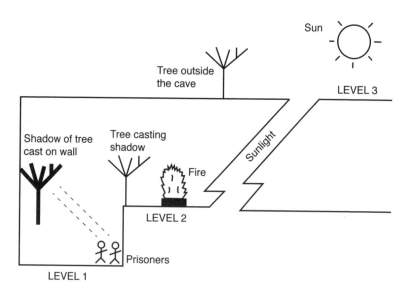

Figure 1. Plato's Allegory of the Cave

are cast on the wall in front of them, which are the only things that they can see. They cannot see the fire behind them, nor the things held up to the fire that cause the shadows. As they can only see the shadows, and have no reason to think there is anything beyond them, the prisoners think that they are seeing real things, whereas we can see that they only see shadows.

In Plato's model, we have three layers of reality. We have the shadows on the wall, which represent how things are appearing to the prisoners in the cave. We can call this reality level 1, *appearance*, as it is the way things appear to be to the prisoners. Next we have the movements of the things casting the shadows. This is more real than the shadows, as the appearance of the shadows is dependent upon the movement of the things, so we can call this reality level 2, *reality behind the appearance*. Finally, there is an additional layer of reality which is independent of both of these levels: the ultimate reality that is found outside the cave itself. We can call this reality level 3, *true reality*.

The pro wrestling version of Plato's Cave can be represented as shown in figure 2.

Let's start with the fans. The action as it's presented in the ring is what the audience is intended to see, and is the show taken at face value. This is reality level 1. It's this level of reality that the term "kayfabe" refers to, and when people talk about "keeping kayfabe", they're talking about the need to preserve *the appearances*. To do this, pro wrestlers used to keep in character outside of shows, and wrestlers feuding with one another on screen weren't allowed to be seen in public together.

Next, we have the first layer behind the appearance of the match as presented, which is the work of the wrestlers in the ring. According to appearances, we have people who are hurting each other with

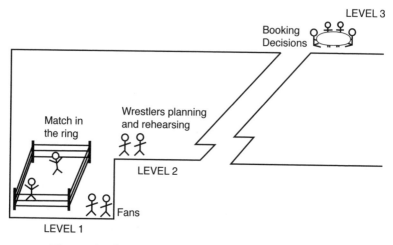

Figure 2. Plato's Allegory applied to Pro Wrestling

elaborate moves, and who are engaged in a contest. As we know, though, things are not as they seem, as the wrestlers are not engaged in a contest to win the match, and the moves they are performing are not performed in order to hurt each other (indeed, if performed well, they should not hurt to the extent they are portrayed to). The wrestlers themselves, and the way they jointly perform the match, project an image of what is happening, namely a genuine athletic contest with genuine intent to harm, which is not what is really happening. This is reality level 2. Interest in this level of reality will involve questions like "how did they do that?", when considering how a particular move is pulled off. To find out more about this, you might go to a wrestling school.

Finally, we have reality level 3, which is the reality ultimately responsible for the other layers. In pro wrestling, this is the realm of the bookers and promoters who write the storylines, and determine the outcomes of the matches. This comes about as we can ask the question of why the performers are doing what they're doing at level

2, and why they're subsequently portraying the appearances at level 1. In pro wrestling, it's typically because each match showcases not only the wrestlers' athletic ability, but also their skill as actors telling a particular story. The story is written by the bookers, and they will give guidance to the performers which enables them to act the story out in a cohesive way.

The realm of the bookers is thus the "ultimate reality" of pro wrestling. When we ask why certain things happened, we typically hit bedrock when we consider the decisions of those booking the matches and the shows. This is the way to "escape the cave", using the analogy above, as it is to uncover true reality. This mirrors the purpose of Plato's original allegory of the cave, which was to illustrate the difficulties we human beings have in knowing things about the world around us. For Plato, in our everyday lives we are like the prisoners, only having access to the evidence of our senses, which we cannot break away from. The experience we have is of objects in the world that present themselves to us in certain ways, but we can never see *the things themselves*, just our individual perceptions of them. We also have no idea what reality is fundamentally like; what the origins of these things are.

The philosopher's quest, for Plato, is to escape the cave, and the bounds of our senses, by attaining knowledge of true reality through rational inquiry. Likewise, the pro wrestling fan's quest is to escape the cave by getting knowledge of the true reality of the backstage decisions behind the shows as presented. Let's now examine more closely the relationships between these levels of reality.

2. Reality Intrusions

Some of the most thrilling moments for wrestling fans are the moments when the reality behind the appearances breaks through, giving the viewer a glimpse of the real world behind the show. These moments, called "shoots", are not part of the show; they are times when something unplanned happens, or something happens that at least one of the performers is unaware of. Perhaps the most infamous moment of this kind in contemporary wrestling history is the "Montreal Screwjob", which had a major role in changing the way pro wrestling was perceived by both performers and fans.

The essentials of the story are as follows. It is the WWF in 1997. Since the rise of WCW, the WWF is facing serious competition for the first time in a while. The WWF champion is Bret "Hitman" Hart, a WWF mainstay since the late 1980s. From the legendary Hart wrestling family in Calgary, Hart is an exceptional technical wrestler, wearing distinctive pink and black ring attire. He is a former two-time Tag Team Champion, two-time Intercontinental Champion, King of the Ring Winner, and five-time WWF Champion, and has been involved in some of the most memorable matches in the company's history. Hart started as part of the heel tag team "the Hart Foundation", with his brother-in-law Jim "the Anvil" Neidhart. Gradually, the Hart Foundation turned babyface, and Hart set out on a singles career. He won the Intercontinental Championship, followed by the WWF Championship, and was a classic babyface: a loyal, never-say-die underdog, who was a clear fan favorite.

However, during his feud with Stone Cold Steve Austin in late 1996/early 1997, the fans began to tire of Hart's character, turning to Austin instead. The decision was made to turn Hart heel at WrestleMania 13, and Hart took on a new persona, which emphasized his Canadian roots, and launched an anti-American crusade. He won the WWF title from the Undertaker at SummerSlam 1997, and was headed for a collision course with his long-term, and real-life, nemesis, Shawn Michaels at Survivor Series 1997, in Montreal. Hart had long been courted by the rival WCW organization, and finally agreed to accept an offer from them when the WWF failed to offer a serious reason to persuade him to stay. Vince McMahon, the owner of the WWF, had decided that he couldn't afford to keep Hart on the books at a price to compete with the WCW offer, and elected to let Hart go.

The problem was, though, that Hart was still the WWF champion. McMahon's plan was to have Hart lose the title to Michaels in Montreal in his final WWF match. This is normal practice for a wrestler leaving an organization: to "do the honours" on their way out. However, Hart refused to lose to Michaels in Canada, arguing that it would destroy his character, and, given that he had a degree of creative control in his contract, McMahon couldn't force him to do so.

McMahon's solution was ingenious yet dastardly, and hugely controversial. McMahon agreed to a finish to the match with Hart that would see the match end in a disqualification due to interference from both Hart's allies and Michaels's allies. Hart would leave Montreal as champion, and then surrender the title the next night on Monday Night Raw. McMahon then double-crossed Hart by calling from ringside for the match to be ended during a pre-planned spot where Michaels had Hart trapped in his own submission hold, the sharpshooter. The agreed-upon next step was for Hart to reverse the move, holding Michaels in the sharpshooter, before the promised interference would occur. However, McMahon, who was at ringside, called for the bell to ring signifying the end of the match while Hart was still trapped in the hold. The impression given was that Hart had submitted, which would have been a humiliating way for him to lose

– to his hated rival, to his own hold, in his own country. Michaels was given the belt and ushered away while Hart stood visibly confused in the ring.

Hart's confusion soon turned to anger, and he spat in McMahon's face, before tearing up the broadcast equipment at ringside, and drawing the letters "WCW" in the air with his finger. Backstage, the drama continued, culminating in Hart punching McMahon in the face, and knocking him out. Remarkably, there was a documentary crew following Hart during this time, and they captured much of this on tape, shown in the documentary *Hitman Hart: Wrestling with Shadows* (leading some to speculate that this whole thing was a work after all!).

This was a key moment where reality entered the wrestling business. Hart's bewildered reaction was not put on, it was his *genuine reaction* to what had happened. McMahon's orders at ringside were not part of the script; they were the result of the owner of the company demanding that a certain outcome be portrayed. By stepping outside of conventional storyline activity, the WWF had exposed a part of pro wrestling that had previously been very carefully kept under wraps: that outcomes to matches were pre-determined, and that the wrestlers knew who was winning. What had exposed this was a clear case when things did *not* go as one wrestler thought they would, and it was so clear that it had to be addressed. Interestingly, instead of trying to cover it up, the WWF leant straight into it, with McMahon addressing the issue directly in a subsequent interview on Monday Night Raw. Here is what McMahon said:

> Some would say I screwed Bret Hart. Bret Hart would definitely tell you I screwed him. I look at it from a different standpoint. I look at it from the standpoint of the referee did not screw Bret Hart. Shawn Michaels certainly did not screw Bret Hart. Nor did

Vince McMahon screw Bret Hart. I truly believe that Bret Hart screwed Bret Hart. And he can look in the mirror and know that.

I will certainly take responsibility for any decision I ever made, I never had a problem doing that. Not all of my decisions are accurate, they're not. But when I make a bad decision, I'm not above saying that I'm sorry and trying to do the best about it that I can. Hopefully the batting average is pretty good, I make more good decisions than I do bad decisions. And as far as screwing Bret Hart is concerned, there's a time-honored tradition in the wrestling business, that when someone is leaving that they show the right amount of respect to the superstars, in this case to the people that made you that superstar. I mean you show the proper respect to the organization that helped you become who you are today. It's a time-honored tradition and Bret Hart didn't want to honor that tradition.

That's something I would have never ever expected from Bret, because he's known somewhat as a traditionalist in this business. It would have never crossed my mind that Bret wouldn't want to show the right amount of respect to the superstars that helped make him and the organization that helped make him what he is today. I know that was Bret's decision. Bret screwed Bret. (WWF Raw is War, 11/17/19, *WWE Network*)

Here McMahon is clearly implying – if not outright stating – that Bret Hart caused the problems for himself because he refused to do what was expected of him by the "time-honored tradition" of the wrestling business, namely lose when you are leaving. This would obviously lead the fan to ask, "well, if there are some circumstances when wrestlers know they will lose, why is this not always the case?" And, once you've been "smartened up" to the wrestling business, it is hard to go back and view it in the way you did beforehand. This moment is thought by many to be the final nail in the coffin of "kayfabe"; the moment when the wrestling business stopped pretending that wrestlers were really fighting each other. Even if many fans had worked it out, it hadn't been acknowledged by a wrestling company on air in such an explicit way. Breaking kayfabe represented a risk for McMahon, as it could have caused the audience to change the way they engaged with pro wrestling, and not necessarily in a positive way.

What it did instead was explicitly acknowledge an area of intrigue that had fascinated a sub-section of the pro wrestling audience, namely those interested in the "true reality" of pro wrestling: the activity of promoters and bookers at the management level. Let's think more about this, and what it tells us about the relationship between appearance and reality.

3. Dirt Sheets, Podcasts, and *Total Divas*: The Quest for Reality

The Montreal Screwjob came at a time when reality had gradually seeped its way into pro wrestling storylines. Gone (mostly) were the outlandish and colorful characters and storylines that had populated the late 1980s and early 1990s, with wrestling companies realizing that fans in the late 1990s wanted something more reality-based. Gone were the halcyon days of the pro wrestling "gimmicks", where wrestlers had to be given some other profession to give themselves a character, such as a tax collector, clown, dentist, or barber. Instead, characters became generally more based on the real people that played them, with the wrestlers becoming extended versions of themselves, as opposed to completely different characters. Even the most legendary gimmick of all – the WWF's Undertaker – would be updated to reflect the real person playing the character, transforming from a zombie mortician into a biker.

This more reality-based approach was precipitated by Eric Bischoff's New World Order (nWo) storyline in WCW, which had led to WCW overtaking the WWF in the Monday night TV ratings war. This was pitched initially as an "invasion" of WCW by two former WWF wrestlers, Scott Hall and Kevin Nash, who had wrestled as Razor Ramon and Diesel in the WWF. The invasions on WCW Monday Nitro were presented as unscripted events, with Hall's debut coming when he emerged in street clothes from the crowd while a match was taking place in the ring. Hall and Nash cut promos using backstage wrestling terminology, and the commentators pretended not to know what was going on. This presented a degree of intrigue for the fans: was this a *real* WWF invasion of WCW? Were Hall and Nash just showing up and doing whatever they wanted? The chaotic nature of the shows suggested that nobody knew what was going on, and anything could happen at any moment.

The success of this storyline, propelling WCW to previously-unheard-of heights of success for the company, showed that fans were ready for a presentation of pro wrestling that cut much closer to reality than had ever been done before.

Cutting close to reality has generally brought success in the pro wrestling business. The nWo storyline suggests that, as do the successes of storylines that play on real-life feelings and events, such as the Matt Hardy-Edge-Lita feud of the 2000s, which drew on a real-life love triangle, and the CM Punk "pipebomb" promo of 2011, where Punk spoke on live WWE TV about his dissatisfaction with the company. Indeed, the idea of a "worked-shoot" became something prominent in the pro wrestling business, where something is set up (a work), but is presented as something unplanned and real (a shoot). The idea is to captivate fans who will preoccupy themselves with the question, "was that meant to happen?", thus generating interest in the event. This strategy remains popular, and was employed at one of the biggest shows of 2019 – the G1 Supercard at Madison Square Garden – where former WWE wrestlers Enzo and Big Cass jumped the guardrail and began attacking Ring of Honor tag teams after a match. I was there in the crowd and the buzz it generated in the audience at the time was palpable; for a while all I could hear around me was people discussing whether it was a work or a shoot.

This thirst for backstage knowledge drives a secondary industry in the wrestling business. Started by "dirt sheets" like Dave Meltzer's influential *Wrestling Observer Newsletter*, much of contemporary wrestling shows have been accompanied by journalistic appraisals of the product which also features insider gossip and rumors about the reality behind the appearances: why was this character booked this way? Do these wrestlers *really* dislike one another? Why did the company choose to back this wrestler over another one? Whose idea was this angle? Did this wrestler have a problem losing this match? The advent of the internet evidently increased this interest, and the sheer number of pro wrestling podcasts now add to this body of information. Many of these, such as Conrad Thompson's *Something to Wrestle with Bruce Prichard, What Happened When with Tony Schiavone*, and *83 Weeks with Eric Bischoff*, feature influential figures from the pro wrestling backrooms of the past, giving tell-all accounts of what *really* happened during many of the most influential moments in pro wrestling history.

In terms of contemporary pro wrestling, the situation is even more peculiar. For one thing, companies like WWE now have numerous "behind the scenes" shows which expose the people behind the characters in ways not previously seen. Shows like *Total Divas, Total Bellas*, and *Miz and Mrs* are regularly shown on cable TV channels, and WWE's own WWE Network features numerous shows where pro wrestlers are featured in their "real lives" outside of the shows. In addition to this, most pro wrestlers have their own social media accounts, which include a curious mixture of storyline-based interactions with other pro wrestlers, real-life posts, and blurred lines between the two.

This is the explicit commodification of the quest for reality motivation discussed above: fans are keen to know what's really happening behind the scenes, and who really likes and dislikes each other, and such shows and social media accounts purportedly give access to this. WWE has noticed the potential for expanding their product in this way, and jumped on it, entering markets like reality TV to extend their fanbase. This may suggest that pro wrestling gives us something: clear access to the reality behind the appearances. If you want to know what *really* happened at a particular show, just find the right podcast episode, or watch the right reality TV show, and you'll know. Escaping the cave is as easy as plugging in your headphones or turning on your TV.

However, things are not so simple. Some of the key principles of the pro wrestling business are *work* the audience, *entertain* the audience, *sell* your product to the audience. The reality-based products are not there simply for the sake of it; they are also selling something. They are also designed to be entertaining. They are not simply put there as a public service to give the audience an insight into what really happened: they are designed to entertain and promote, in different ways. A lot of the time, this is because the intrigue is just a lot more interesting than the unvarnished truth. As Sean Oliver puts it in his book *Kayfabe: Stories You're Not Supposed to Hear from a Pro Wrestling Production Company Owner*:

I've read fans' posts that take issue with a wrestler's version or recollection of past events. Is it a lie detector we need? Or maybe a star's version of events is far more interesting than the neutral, lukewarm truth. (Oliver 2017: 150)

What a fan with a critical eye must consider is whether these "reality-based" products *are* giving us reality, or whether they are instead just another level of appearance.

Think about, for example, a show like *Total Bellas*. When you're watching this, are you getting an insight into the *real life* of Brie and Nikki Bella, or are you getting a *presentation* of their real life? Even if *real stuff* is happening, like Nikki Bella and John Cena breaking up, or Brie Bella and Daniel Bryan having a child, are you getting the *real* reactions of the people, or are you getting a particular version of those people, carefully curated to make for an interesting television show? Even the fact that this question is difficult to answer suggests that it's not so clear that we are getting clear access to reality.

With podcasts, while we are presented with the idea that they are tell-all exposés of what really happened, they are also designed to be entertaining. For instance, on *Something to Wrestle with Bruce Prichard*, both Prichard and the host, Conrad Thompson, emphasize that the show is intended for entertainment purposes, and that some of what is said is not to be taken literally. Whilst undoubtedly much of what's said is intended to be a legitimate representation of Prichard's memories of events, the fact that we know that some is not muddies the waters in respect to this being an insight into true reality, as opposed to another form of appearance. Other "behind-the-scenes" shows have copped to working moments that are presented as shoots, such as *Kayfabe Commentaries* engineering a physical altercation between the Iron Sheik and B. Brian Blair at a comedy roast of the Iron Sheik.

Perhaps what this tell us is that, whenever we are presented with something that seems like true reality, by the very act of our ability to access it, we are also able to ask questions about it. One of these is the question of whether this *really* is true reality, or whether there is something deeper underneath. As a consequence, we might wonder whether we can really ever *know* what true reality is like. If, whenever we are presented with what may be true reality, we can also ask whether it really *is* true reality, we seem hamstrung in our ability to know whether we have really accessed true reality.

In addition to this, there is still disagreement between particular people about "what really happened". On a memorable episode of *83 Weeks with Eric Bischoff* about Bret Hart's time in WCW, Bischoff vigorously disputed a number of claims made by Hart himself in Hart's autobiography. We – as listeners – just have Bischoff's claims and Hart's claims to go by, and we must decide who is correct about what really happened. But how can we do this? Such disagreement again further calls into question whether we really get access to reality in this way, or whether we get another form of exaggerated, or emphasized, reality, designed to entertain rather than present facts. (Indeed, the presence of vigorous disagreement fits with Bischoff's "controversy creates cash" slogan, the title of his 2006 book.)

The same applies to books written by wrestlers recording their experiences throughout their careers. Again, they have two purposes: to give an accurate account of what happened, and to be entertaining. Sometimes it's unclear which of these goals takes priority, and, even though you can usually take it that what's said is in the proximity of truth, you can never really be sure. Also, once again, you only ever get that person's perspective on what happened, which may be colored by their own desires, preconceptions, and feelings about the events.

For example, going back to the Montreal Screwjob, there are a number of conflicting reports of who came up with the idea for the double-cross. Vince McMahon, Shawn Michaels, Triple H, Gerald Brisco, Jim Cornette, and Vince Russo are all people who have either been credited with the idea or claimed responsibility for it at one time or another. As the 2019 Viceland *Dark Side of the Ring* documentary on the Screwjob showed, even now, over 20 years later, whenever one tries to get to the reality underneath, one just uncovers more confusion.

This is not to say that people are trying to mislead, or even that they are not telling the truth, deliberately or otherwise. It is just to say that the presence of conflicting accounts makes it harder for the listener, or reader, to work out what the *true reality* is. Rather than bringing the fan closer to that, they can often leave them just as much in the dark as they were before.

4. The Co-Dependence of Reality and Appearance

Maybe, though, this isn't so much of a problem. When we look for reality, we do really want to know what happened, but we also want the story to continue. The best "tell-all" accounts are those that settle some questions, but also raise others, prompting new speculation and intrigue. Our quest for reality is not so much about *reality* as it is about the *quest*.

We can see this by looking at what happened when pro wrestling *did* try to just be about reality, and lost sight of something key: *appearances*. In 1999, WCW was floundering after its success of the late 1990s, and brought in WWF writer Vince Russo to try to turn the tide. Russo's approach was to push this reality-based idea to the max, and bring the scripted element of wrestling explicitly to the forefront in the way the show was presented. He presented himself onscreen as a "writer", and wrestlers were booked to perform in a way that directly exposed the scripted nature of wrestling, such as Buff Bagwell refusing to lose a match, and Jeff Jarrett laying down for Hulk Hogan. Russo was trying to play on the success of reality-based storylines by presenting *just the reality* (or, at least the reality as intended to be presented), without the pretense that pro wrestling was anything other than scripted entertainment. This was not an unreasonable approach given the success that reality-based storylines had enjoyed, but it ended up tanking, and WCW went out of business not long after.

What this suggests is that the interest and intrigue in pro wrestling is not *just* about the reality; it is also about the interplay between the reality and the *appearance*. In the mid-1990s, wrestling companies realized that people were sick of just appearances; they needed a dose of reality. Russo's WCW showed that fans weren't interested in *just* the reality, though. They wanted the appearance so that they could speculate, discuss, and theorize about the reality: if you strip the appearances away entirely, then this removes the interest. I think it's also fair to say that they wanted the appearance because they enjoyed it. Wrestling fans enjoy suspending disbelief to get into and appreciate a good feud, or match, even if afterwards they will pick it apart and look for the tells of the reality behind it. This is part of what it is to appreciate the drama and art of pro wrestling, and if you remove that, you remove an essential aspect of the activity's appeal.

We talked before about how pro wrestling provides a way to think about the distinction between appearance and reality, and we can now see that it tells us something important about the relationship between them, and the role it has in our lives. We often want to know what's real: are things the way I see them to be; what *really* happened that day; or what do people *really* think of each other? We search for reality both by ourselves and discussing with others: indeed, much of our conversations with others involve gossip, speculation about what's really going on with people we know. Of course, we *want* to know all this stuff, but we also enjoy the intrigue; the speculation. If we remove the appearances and *just* have reality, then all of this intrigue, speculation, and investigation disappears too. We lose a lot of stuff that matters to us. It is a curious thing that we seem to need both the drive for reality, and also the things that obscure it.

This is not always a positive thing. Some say to never let the truth get in the way of a good story, and that quest for a good story is exactly what we're talking about. The more this permeates our general culture, though, the less truth gets a look in. The more boring the reality is, the less people want to settle for believing it: *surely there's something more interesting there*. This is how conspiracy theories get started: it may be that it's more interesting to think that the moon landing was a hoax. More worryingly, it may be that it makes a better story to explain people's poverty by talking about invading hordes of immigrants coming in and taking what's rightfully theirs. None of this is true, but it takes root in people's minds because it makes for a good story: there is intrigue, speculation, an attempted "cover up" to mask the reality of the situation. I'll leave further examples to you. But sometimes reality is boring. Sometimes there is no intrigue. And sometimes we need to force ourselves to be content with this. Otherwise our cultural dialogues become more like pro wrestling storylines than they should.

5. Pro Wrestling, News Media, and Democracy

As Eric Bischoff points out in a 2018 Tedx talk, we can extend many ideas about pro wrestling to the media more generally: newspaper companies are trying to sell newspapers; news websites are trying to get you to click through. They are all trying to *sell* something. Different websites will present the same events in different ways, depending on their particular slant, and their particular audiences. Trying to work out the reality of a situation in any sphere now is incredibly daunting due to the sheer variety of different perspectives available. Bischoff claims that the news media now focuses more on eliciting emotion from its viewers or readers, as this is the thing that will captivate them, and encourage them to consume more news. This is much like the methods of pro wrestling promoters, who aim to get their audiences emotionally involved to keep them watching and attending shows.

Here again we see the desire to *feel entertained*, to *feel intrigued* being prized over simply thinking what is true. By being presented as a form of entertainment, news – whether on TV or the internet – is not necessarily always in the game of presenting cold, clear, facts. News programs on TV need to attract viewers; news websites need clicks, which means they have to do things to attract the attention of their consumers. If the truth alone is boring, then they need to find ways to make it more interesting, which sometimes may mean leaving the truth out of the picture altogether.

Part of this need to attract an audience means playing to your audience's sympathies. Just as pro wrestling companies need compelling characters that an audience can relate to, news companies need to pitch their shows in ways that the audience will react positively to. One way to do this is to take a page right out of the pro wrestling playbook and pitch one side as the babyface, and the other as the heel. Indeed, this is what you typically see, with different channels taking different sides. For example, in the United States, on MSNBC, the Democrats are the babyfaces, and the Republicans the heels; on FOX News, the Republicans are the babyfaces, and the Democrats the heels. You watch the show that you will enjoy watching the most, which is likely to be the one that aligns with your own views about who the good guys and bad guys are. It is uncomfortable, and sometimes distressing, to watch the other channel, so why do that? This plays into the increasing polarization of political views, where you just seek out the information that reinforces your own perspective, as opposed to looking for a balance of both sides of the issue. This seeps into views about the world more generally, as seen by the prominence of climate change deniers and anti-vaxxers in the US, where there is a distrust of the scientific methods usually trusted to deliver the sorts of things we might class as objective facts.

This is a dangerous situation for a democratic society, where informed, reasoned, debate ought to form the cornerstone of the system. Interestingly, I think wrestling fans, particularly "smart" wrestling fans, may point us towards a way of responding to this situation in a positive and productive way. Wrestling fans are dedicated, informed, relentless in their pursuit of the truth about a particular issue, and they hate being told what to think by wrestling companies. One of the challenges WWE has had in the past few years is how to keep its audience engaged, as they often react very negatively to the stars that WWE wants to push as their main babyfaces, such as John Cena and Roman Reigns. Fans don't see what WWE wants them to see, and are willing to call bullshit on their attempts to push them to the moon. Here, an interest in the subject – pro wrestling – transcends the perceived need to respond as a promotion wants you to respond: you have the power to reject what the company is pushing, even if you still love the company itself. Wrestling fans hold wrestling companies *accountable* for what they do, which is a really important fact that we should not lose sight of.

Now think about people responding to the news in this way. Even if you have your favorite news company, the idea is that you're not pre-disposed to accept whatever they are telling you. You have a commitment, a passion, for something beyond this particular company – the news, or truth, in this case – and that is more important to you than any particular story that the company is pushing. If that story doesn't work, you'll call bullshit on it, and reject what the company is doing. Acting like a wrestling fan when it comes to news would be to hold news companies *accountable*, which is exactly what is required in a democratic society.

Another key feature of smart wrestling fans is the relentless pursuit of the truth. When fans become interested in why a particular event occurred, they will do all they can to get to the bottom of it. As noted above, this desire for reality is what drives the side-industry of dirt sheets, podcasts, and documentaries. This is another instance of what we should expect from journalists, and from citizens, of democracies: the willingness to pursue truth relentlessly, and to go down various rabbit holes in search of the facts. Sometimes this is painted as obsessive in regard to wrestling fans, but it should not be seen in a negative way. It is an example of how all of us should be prepared to act when it comes to the news: we should be prepared to spend time and effort uncovering what really happened; take time to read various sources; be prepared to question what those in powerful positions are saying; and be able to reach our own informed judgments about what happened.

Wrestling companies know that it is hard to pull one over on smart fans; and they also know that they have to work really hard if they are to get their allegiance. They also know that they have to treat them with respect, and not act as if they are stupid or gullible. They know that they will be held accountable if they screw up, and that it is dangerous to ignore their voices. The wrestling company–smart fan relationship is not a million miles away from what you'd like the relationship between government and citizen to be in a democracy, and one way to address the problems we find with democracy now would be to take some cues from smart wrestling fans. In other words, to go back to Plato's Cave, we shouldn't rest content with appearances – we must seek the reality beyond them.

2

Freedom: Scripting vs Spontaneity

We've looked at the distinction between appearance and reality, and how pro wrestling can help us get a handle on the idea. We will now turn to a specific application of this idea, which concerns an apparent distinction between pro wrestling and real life. This is the idea that pro wrestling is scripted, whereas real life is not, which makes pro wrestling somehow less real, or, to use the dreaded f-word, "fake". Closer examination of this idea, however, will reveal that this distinction is much less clear-cut than it is often thought to be, and the freedom we think we experience in "real" life is closer to being scripted than we might think it is.

1. Scripts and Freedom

One of the key lines of thought in the "wrestling is fake" narrative is the view that pro wrestling is scripted. Wrestlers are not acting freely in the way that a football player or a tennis player does on the field or the court; they are acting in accordance with a script that has been set out by a booker, or a road agent. This is not always accurate, as some wrestlers improvise a lot more than they are given credit for, but there are still general rules that they have to follow that are determined by the script. Not only does the script determine the outcome of the match, but it also determines *how* a wrestler should act and carry themselves in general: if you're a babyface you play fair, and respect the crowd; if you're a heel, you cheat and disrespect the crowd. Wrestlers are scripted to have the personalities they have, and their actions are, to a large extent, determined by this.

This can lead to a lot of frustration from viewers. Think about the controversy in 2016–18 surrounding the Roman Reigns character in WWE. He was presented by the company as a babyface, overcoming challenging odds. However, many fans did not respond well to this presentation, and booed Roman Reigns to the point where – judging by his crowd reactions – you would think he was a heel. What the fans wanted was for Reigns to embrace this and turn heel – to explicitly talk trash about the fans and embrace the heel role. However, the company wouldn't do this, and kept pushing him as a babyface (or as an ambiguous character), seemingly with the hope that the fans would eventually start cheering him. Here the fans desperately wanted Reigns to break free of his written role, but he couldn't, and whilst the fans' anger seemed directed toward him, it was really directed toward the writers who refused to change his scripted role.

This is in stark contrast to real life, right? When we go about our daily lives, we are not following a script which states how we should or shouldn't act – it's all up to us. We are not acting out a role when we go about our business, we are just being ourselves, which is precisely not what pro wrestlers are doing. Moreover, when we are frustrated with someone's behavior, we are frustrated *with them*, and their unwillingness to act differently – we see them as responsible for what they do, unlike pro wrestling where we can legitimately be frustrated with those writing the scripts, as in the Roman Reigns example.

So, this seems to be a key dimension where pro wrestling differs from real life, and allows us to get a handle on the difference between "real" and "fake". However, when we think about "real life" in more detail, we see that the differences are not as clear as they appear to be.

2. Scripting and Coaching in Sports

First of all, to anticipate our discussion of sports in chapter 6, it is not clear that what we find in pro wrestling is all that different from other sports. Think about instructions that players get from coaches. It is very unusual for a player to take the field, or the court, without *any* instruction on the sorts of things they are expected to do. This can take various forms, of different levels of strictness. For instance, a tennis player may be given general instructions to implement in a number of different circumstances, such as "play to the opponent's backhand", where a general strategy is given for the player to follow as they see fit as the match progresses. Alternatively, in sports such as American Football, in each play players are given *very* specific instructions about what they should do: the quarterback must throw the ball to a particular player; the tight end must run a very specific line; the members of the offensive line are given specific players to block, and so on. In this case in particular, the difference between scripted and "free" action looks very hard to discern. The players have to use their judgment when it comes to implementing the play, but once the play is decided by the coach, they have very little choice about what they will do.

The main difference between American Football plays and pro wrestling matches is that, in wrestling matches, *both* wrestlers are part of the same play, as it were: they are working together to implement a game plan dictated by the bookers. Whether or not the play comes off is down to their skill in implementing it, with the additional variable not being an opposing team, but the audience's willingness to participate in the event. Note, though, that this is not a difference in terms of the *scripting* of the behavior of those involved: in both cases the participants' behavior is scripted, and there is just a difference in the variables that can prevent the script from coming off.

This is even more apparent when we consider the similarities between pro wrestling and performance-based sports, such as gymnastics, ice skating, diving, and synchronized swimming, to be explored later on. In these sports there is an explicit script to follow – a routine – which is set out by the athlete and their coach, and the success of the performance is judged in terms of how successful the execution of the script is. In pro wrestling the terms are different – we have the agent for the match instead of the coach – but the principles are the same. In many cases, the wrestlers and the agent agree upon a plan for the match, and discuss how the match will progress, and which spots follow others, leading to the finish of the match. The wrestlers' job is then to go out and execute that plan. There seems to be little difference between this procedure and the way the performance-based sports noted above proceed.

What's also key in regular sports is the balance between coaching and player spontaneity. Sometimes teams are criticized for being "over-coached", in that they rely too much on pre-planned coaching routines, and the players do not have the creative ability to react on the fly to situations that come up. This is a criticism routinely leveled at rugby union teams since the game went professional, and at football teams coached by José Mourinho. In sports there needs to be a good balance between coaching plans and player freedom. Interestingly, this is a balance we also see in pro wrestling, and exploring it will take us further into the importance of freedom.

3. Degrees of Scripting

The *degree* to which pro wrestling is scripted is something that varies considerably depending on the kind of promotion. Some promotions give the wrestlers a broad outline of what they want done in a match, or a promo, and then let the wrestlers exercise their own creative abilities in developing and executing. Others, most notably WWE for the last 15 years or so, have teams of writers and match agents heavily scripting every single aspect of the shows. This gives the wrestlers themselves a lot less leeway in what they do than in other promotions, which on occasion leads to a significant amount of discontent.

For example, in 2019 the WWE wrestler Dean Ambrose, now known as Jon Moxley, decided not to renew his WWE contract and work for independent promotions outside of WWE instead. This was a relatively unheard of move for a top star to make, due to WWE being the only mainstream wrestling company in the United States at the time. Usually, the flow goes the other way around: people work hard on the independent scene to get a shot at a WWE contract, and, once there, the money and exposure is so significant that few want to leave. Moxley's reasons for leaving, though, were explicitly tied to a desire for freedom, which may seem paradoxical in the context of pro wrestling. Let's explore the situation in more detail.

In an interview with Chris Jericho on the *Talk is Jericho* podcast in May 2019, Moxley and Jericho discussed the creative process in WWE, and Moxley's frustrations with it. A key issue for Moxley was that WWE, with their teams of writers and producers headed by Vince McMahon, carefully script every promo, and structure every match, which leaves the wrestlers with little scope to put their own stamp on things. Moxley describes his feelings on a writer, conveying notes received from Vince McMahon on his performance as follows:

Jon Moxley: "Notes from VKM [Vince McMahon]: Dean needs to understand why he needs to insult the audience. Dean needs to read his promos verbatim and not try to re-write them." And I'm just like [long sigh]. Just like the feeling of getting punched in the gut like what the . . . And I said to the writer, it's not his fault, but I yelled at him. He just took the brunt of it. I'm like, Why do I work here? I'm a professional wrestler who can tell stories and come up with promos and I believe that I have the ability to talk people into buildings, I learned those skills years ago and wanted to bring them here to WWE and you just want me to say your stupid lines. If you want somebody to read your stupid lines, hire an actor. Cause they'll probably do a better job of it than me. I'm not interested in doing it.

Moxley goes on to discuss the effect that a steady flow of such events had on him:

Moxley: It's almost like, over the years, like a physical depression sets in. 'Cause they take away the thing that you love. Like I was saying, being obsessed with wrestling 24/7, it's like they take it away from you. "Oh, don't worry about coming up with your own promos, we have a writer. Don't worry about coming up with cool things to do in your matches, 'cause we have producers who will tell exactly what to do in your matches. Don't bother thinking of storylines, 'cause we've already written 'em for you."
Chris Jericho: Don't be an artist and be creative.
Moxley: Don't worry – we've taken care of everything! You just show up. So you're just like oh, okay. So what do I do in my off-time? What do I have to think about? Uh . . . so you try to fill it with other things, and that's a recipe for a very unhappy person.

A very unfulfilled existence. (Transcription from cagesideseats.
com)

Moxley's frustration and unhappiness at working in WWE boils down
to a lack of freedom: in this case, a lack of *creative* freedom to come up
with and execute his own ideas for his character. By rigidly demanding that he follow the script, WWE took away Moxley's freedom to
create, which, for him, was a key element of his job, and which made it
enjoyable and worthwhile to him. Elsewhere in the interview, Moxley
makes the analogy with being in a prison cell, and it's no surprise that
the video Moxley made promoting his move away from WWE was of
a man pacing in a prison cell, counting the days on the wall, and then
breaking out. His first T-shirt after leaving was emblazoned with the
slogan "Unscripted Violence".

It's important to distinguish here between *creative freedom* and
creative control. *Creative freedom* is when a wrestler is able to come up
with their own ideas to execute the broad plan that the promotion has
given them for a match or promo. For instance, the promotion might
say to a wrestler: you're wrestling X tonight, you have 20 minutes.
You're winning, but make X look good. It's then up to the wrestler to
work out how to do this, in their own way. Or, for a promo, they might
be told: you have 3 minutes to build up your match against X. Broad
outline is that X attacked your friend. Then the wrestler has to come
up with what to say to execute this. This gives the wrestler a degree
of creative freedom, as they have a lot of freedom concerning how
they go about doing this. This is in contrast to the situation Moxley
was describing in WWE, where you would not be given broad strokes,
but a detailed script setting out every word of a promo, or have an
agent set out every move of a match, leaving the wrestlers themselves
much less freedom to put their own stamp on things. Nevertheless,

having creative freedom does not imply that you are free to determine whether you win or lose matches, or have control over your storylines, as these are things still set by the promoter.

Creative control, on the other hand, is when a wrestler has power over the storylines they are involved in, and whether they win or lose matches. A wrestler who has a creative control clause in their contract has not just freedom, but *power*, in that they can set the terms for what their character does. They can refuse to lose a match, or engage in a storyline they don't like, and, as a result, essentially become de facto members of the booking team, as key ideas involving them have to be approved by them. Very few wrestlers have had this power, partly because it makes life very difficult – if not untenable – for promoters if wrestlers have this degree of control. Hulk Hogan in WCW is one of the few examples of wrestlers who had creative control for an extended period, and this is often given as one reason WCW ultimately failed to survive. Sometimes wrestlers, like Ric Flair and Kevin Nash in WCW, are asked to join the booking team while still active wrestlers, becoming sort of player-managers if you will, but this is not quite the same thing as having a contract with creative control built in.

What Moxley was unhappy about in WWE was not the lack of creative *control*, but the lack of creative *freedom*. For many wrestlers, it's not about having control over who wins and who loses, as this is not really what being a wrestler is about, but rather about having the ability to perform as you see fit, and to develop your character and your wrestling style as you see fit. Even in the scripted world of pro wrestling, freedom is important. Many performers desire, and need, a significant degree of freedom if they are to do their jobs properly.

This exposes another dimension of why the "wrestling is fake" narrative is fundamentally misguided. This desire for freedom, for authenticity in your performance, is a desire for something as real as anything else. What frustrated Moxley was the inability to express his very real and authentic creativity in his performances, and this obstruction of his creativity led to him losing interest in what he was doing. It started to feel "goofy", and "hokey" to him – his character ceased to become believable to him, and *that,* no doubt, felt fake, but this is not because wrestling as a whole is fake, but because he was put in a position where he was unable to perform in a genuine way.

OK, but what about the hyper-scripted world of WWE in 2019: is *this* fake, even if wrestling as a whole is not? It certainly seems *more* fake, in that the performers are not able to exercise genuine creative freedom, but is it *wholly* fake? This seems hard to justify, as the fact that something is scripted, even if down to the minutest detail, doesn't normally warrant it being called "fake". Think of scripted movies or TV shows, for example: these are not thought of as fake, even though every word spoken, and every action taken, is scripted. There is still *some* creative freedom: otherwise why are some actors considered better than others? – It's not all mechanical. The same is true of WWE: even if it is heavily scripted, there is still *some* creative freedom in terms of how performers deliver their lines, or execute a match. Some wrestlers are still better than others, even in this context, so something real still shines through the scripted structure.

4. The Wrestling Stoic

Even with this idea of creative freedom in play, we might still think that there's a difference between pro wrestling and *real life* in that we are free to do absolutely whatever we like, whereas wrestlers in a show are still following a script, even if it is just broad outlines. Thinking more about this, though, shows that pro wrestling is a much more accurate representation of real life than we might think it is. The idea that real life is as scripted as pro wrestling is expressed in the philosophical problem of free will.

Setting aside those few who have creative control, the life of a pro wrestler seems to be a life characterized by a lack of control. A wrestler does not have control over whether they win or lose, and – to some extent – whether they become a star. These are things determined by powers above their heads, namely the bookers or promoters. They are subject to the whims of these forces, and can merely do the best they can with the opportunities they are given to express themselves.

Put in these terms, the life of a pro wrestler is not a million miles away from how some philosophers called the Stoics thought about human life in general. The Stoics thought that we live in a world where all events are pre-determined by nature. That is, whilst we think we have control over what we do, and what happens to us, we actually don't. The forces that govern the universe are such that they are what determine how things go, and it's only our inflated sense of our own self-importance that makes us think that we play a role in this.

This idea can be played out in different ways, depending on what you take this universal force to be. Some take this force to be God, or Fate, which determines how everything ultimately goes. Others, called "determinists", take it to be something more natural, such as the laws of physics, or the laws of nature. To illustrate, physical events are governed by physical laws that determine the behavior of physical things. Take a pen in your hand, for example. It is a physical thing, and if you drop it – a physical event – it will fall to the floor, as it is governed by physical laws – gravity, in this case. Physical laws don't have exceptions, and determine the way that things behave: the pen has no say in whether it falls to the ground, just as your body has no say about whether it remains rooted to the earth.

Now the thoughts you have, and the decisions you make, are dependent on your brain activity. Your brain is a physical thing – it is an organ made up of cells, that are made up of atoms, and so forth. The goings on inside your brain – a physical thing – are physical events. There is, in theory, no difference *in physical terms* between the neurons firing in your brain which enable you to think, and the pen falling to the ground after it is dropped. Both are physical events, taking place in a physical universe, and they are governed by physical laws. Given that you have no control over these laws, you don't have control over what you think and do.

So, whether we think it's God, Fate, or plain old physics, the idea is that there is some force that is more powerful than us that determines how the events of the universe play out. Whilst we think that we are actors in these events with genuine agency, in fact we are mere spectators.

If this is the case, then our daily lives are determined by a script which is beyond our control, just as a wrestler's actions are determined by a script beyond their control. When we get frustrated at a wrestler's inability to break the script, we are seeing a representation of ourselves, and the difficulties we have in not being able to break the script that determines our own lives. The predicament of pro wrestlers as individuals whose fates are determined by things outside their control reflects the predicament we find ourselves in, subject to the whims of fate.

Whilst this may be an intimidating and somewhat scary idea, the Stoics thought that it was ultimately a way to ease much of the suffering that human beings endure. For instance, a lot of anguish we suffer is from regret: the thought that we could have done something differently than we actually did. Regret is an extremely painful emotion at times, and we can end up torturing ourselves by endlessly analyzing how we could have done things differently. If the Stoics are right, though, regret is an irrational feeling, as, in actual fact, there is no way that things could have gone differently. We *think* that we have control over what we do, and could do things however we want, but in reality we don't: there was only ever one way things were going to go, and we can't control that, just as 2+2 will always equal 4, and there's no way for us to change that.

Rather than torturing ourselves about how things turn out, the Stoics thought that we should find solace by embracing the limits of our freedom, and accepting the fact that we do not control the events of the universe. What we do control, though, are the ways we respond to these events, and by accepting our lack of control, we are better able to be at peace with how things turn out. In other words, by being able to distinguish between what is out of our control (events in the universe), and what is in our control (our reactions to them), the Stoics thought that we can live happier lives. As the Roman philosopher Epictetus puts it in section 1 of his famous *Handbook*:

Some things are in our control and others not. Things in our control are opinion, pursuit, desire, aversion, and, in a word, whatever are our own actions. Things not in our control are body, property, reputation, command, and, in one word, whatever are not our own actions. The things in our control are by nature free, unrestrained, unhindered; but those not in our control are weak, slavish, restrained, belonging to others. Remember, then, that if you suppose that things which are slavish by nature are also free, and that what belongs to others is your own, then you will be hindered. You will lament, you will be disturbed, and you will find fault both with gods and men. But if you suppose that only to be your own which is your own, and what belongs to others such as it really is, then no one will ever compel you or restrain you. Further, you will find fault with no one or accuse no one. You will do nothing against your will. No one will hurt you, you will have no enemies, and you not be harmed.

We can return here to Jon Moxley. A wrestler has little to no control over how they are booked, and the storylines that they are in. What they *do* typically have control over, though, is how they do their promos, and how they perform in their matches. For many, *this* control, this bit of freedom, is what makes it all worthwhile, and what they invest their creative energy in. This is what gives them purpose, and, for some – like Moxley – it is what made them want to be a wrestler in the first place. Even though this freedom is – in the grand scheme of things – pretty minor, it is of vital importance to a wrestler's well-being, just as Epictetus thinks the little bit of freedom of how to respond to things is of vital importance to a person's well-being in general. If it is taken away, it is bound to result in unhappiness and frustration.

There is a key difference, though, which, ironically, would make the fate of pro wrestlers less problematic than our own fates, if the Stoics are correct. As we have talked about, pro wrestlers can "shoot", as in, they can break the script, and perform "real", unscripted actions. Normally, of course, this would result in severe reprimand from their promoter, and few do it, but it doesn't change the fact that they *can* do it. Pro wrestlers have this piece of freedom, even if they typically don't exercise it. If Stoicism is true, though, we don't even have this ability. We are stuck with the script, and are unable to shoot, or break the script, as we are not making a decision to follow it. This would make "real life" even less free than we take pro wrestlers to be.

5. Know Your Role

Let's now set Stoicism aside and consider some different issues. Let's suppose that Stoicism is false, and we do have a degree of control over what we do. Surely now we can confidently say that our actions are more real than wrestlers' actions, as what we do is not scripted, but what they do is?

Unfortunately, things are not so simple here either. There are scripts for many things we do, and many interactions we have. Think about what you're expected to say when you pass someone in the village: "good morning", "have a nice day" – if you don't follow the script you are not interacting with others properly. This can be because you don't say anything, or because you say too much: the script for polite greetings does not involve a detailed and honest answer to "how's it going"? Think also about how annoying it is if someone doesn't say "please" and "thank you": they are not following the script for polite behavior!

There are also general scripts for how our lives are supposed to go. If you are a relatively affluent white male, it might look something like this: you're born, you go to school, you go to college, you get a good job, you get married, you buy a house, you have a couple of kids, you retire, you travel, you downsize, you die. Deviation from the script assigned to you may be met with consternation: what do you mean you don't want to go to college? That's just what you *do* – know your role, and shut your mouth! If you're a woman who decides she doesn't want to have kids, you may feel this a lot: people will ask all sorts of intrusive questions as they are confused and intimidated by the fact that *you're not following the script!*

Scripts are woven into almost every aspect of our lives. Let me describe an average day to you. I get up, take my kid to school, come home, have breakfast with my wife, drive to work, where I teach students, come home, and have dinner with my family. It is tempting to think that there's just me, doing all of those things, and that I don't change as I do them. But notice that I am inhabiting a lot of different roles as I am doing them: a *father*, a *husband*, a *driver*, a *professor*. All of these roles carry expectations for what someone who occupies them should do. A father should act a certain way when dropping their kid off, a husband should behave a certain way toward their spouse, a driver is expected to follow the rules of the road, and a professor is expected to interact with students in a particular way. When I do these things in the course of my day, I am conscious of the behavioral expectations that go with them. And this is just a small sample of the many, many roles we all inhabit: man, woman, child, adult, white person, black person, colleague, customer, American, to name just a few. All of these roles have certain social connotations and behavioral expectations, and they provide many, many different scripts that we are expected to follow.

For example, when my son was younger, I would occasionally take him to the supermarket in his pajamas, particularly in the winter when it was really cold. This was received by other people in a jovial way. However, when my wife did the same thing, she was met with more hostile reactions. A *father* is not expected to be able to dress his child properly, and we can all laugh at his ineptitude, but a *mother* should know better! The dirty looks my wife got were because she was not meeting the social expectations associated with the mother role: she was not following the script!

With scripts comes the idea of *performance*. In our lives, we all have a number of roles that we play, with associated scripts, and we are expected to perform them. This idea is memorably expressed by

Shakespeare in the play *As You Like It,* where the character Jaques says:

> All the world's a stage,
> And all the men and women merely players;
> They have their exits and their entrances;
> And one man in his time plays many parts.

These scripts are particularly relevant when thinking about issues concerning gender, race, and class. There are certain ways that women are *meant* to act, for example, and certain ways that *men* are meant to act. If you don't follow the social scripts, you cause confusion and outrage! These scripts are not really written down, like scripts drawn up by wrestling promoters; instead, they are more the unwritten rules of the societies we live in. The fact that they are not written down, though, does not make them any less powerful, or controlling, or the sanctions for breaking them any less significant. As the philosopher Judith Butler (1988) has explored, this is particularly so with social categories like gender, race, and class, where people are often assigned roles by others, and expected to perform them in accordance with the general social norms associated with them.

The bottom line is that, in our everyday lives, we are following scripts all the time, even if we are not aware that we are doing so. Moreover, we can get frustrated with the scripts, we can get frustrated at other people's judgments of us not following the scripts, and we can get frustrated at other people not following the scripts. "Real life" and pro wrestling are not as different as they might seem. With that in mind, let's look at efforts to flip the script for women in wrestling.

6. Flipping the Script: Women's Wrestling

It's gone midnight at WrestleMania 35. After seven hours of wrestling, the main event is finally here. It's a history-making main event, as it is the first time women have headlined WrestleMania, with Becky Lynch, Charlotte Flair, and Ronda Rousey competing in a triple threat match for both the Raw and SmackDown women's titles. It's taken a long time to get here, to a point where women can main event the biggest show of the year.

It's fair to say that this was not meant to happen, in that the company didn't expect women to headline the event. Traditionally, WrestleMania is headlined by the biggest men's stars, with the men's titles and storylines being the main focus. Even a few short years ago, the idea that women would headline any pay-per-view (PPV), let alone WrestleMania, would have been unthinkable. What made the change was the performers themselves gaining unprecedented fan support in ways the company did not expect, resulting in them breaking the scripts that the company had planned for them, and flipping the established scripts about the respective importance of men's and women's wrestling.

The main catalyst for the WrestleMania main event was Becky Lynch who, after years of floundering as a mid-card babyface, turned heel when she took out her frustrations on her former friend, Charlotte Flair, after Flair won the SmackDown Women's title at SummerSlam 2018. Whilst WWE aimed to present Lynch as a heel, the fans felt differently: they *felt* Lynch's *genuine* frustration at not making it to the top, and embraced her new more aggressive character. This catapulted Lynch to previously unheard-of levels of popularity for a women's wrestler, where she was the person fans most wanted to see. Lynch encapsulated this success with her statement that she was "The Man", which became her new gimmick. This was a claim that she, more than anyone else, was *the* star in the company, *the* best, the main event, *the* person the fans came to see. It also played with the established social scripts about gender nicely, pushing questions about the gendered use of terminology used to denote the top star: "why can't a woman be *the man*?"; and "why assume that *the man* has to be a man?".

Headlining WrestleMania was the triumphant climax of Becky Lynch's transformation into "The Man", helped undoubtedly by her opponents: the mainstream appeal of former UFC Champion Ronda Rousey, and the wrestling excellence of Charlotte Flair made this match impossible to ignore as a main event. To fully appreciate the significance of it, and also to examine where it left women's wrestling going forward, we need to look in a little more detail at the recent history of women's wrestling. For those unfamiliar with this aspect of pro wrestling history, the discussion below, and in the next section on intergender wrestling, includes some disturbing aspects.

This idea of a script was something that hampered women's wrestling for a long time, and to an extent still does. *Women don't fight! Men fight!* This is part of the general script for the behavior of men and women, and pro wrestling cards were structured accordingly. For a long time, women primarily served as valets, or managers for men wrestlers, and as props to be fought over. Women's wrestling was something that was occasionally featured, but these matches were more presented as special attractions rather than central aspects of the shows. In the "Attitude Era" of the late 1990s, women were mainly presented by mainstream American wrestling companies as sex objects, as part of the effort to shift pro wrestling's appeal away from kids to 18–30-year-old men. Characters such as Sable, Sunny, and the "Nitro Girls" were largely there to appear in skimpy outfits and have "we want puppies!" chanted at them by the baying male audience.

Things got worse with the introduction of "bra and panties" matches, where the aim was to strip your opponent to her underwear. These were supplemented in the early 2000s by mud wrestling matches and bikini contests. This is just to skim the surface of the incredibly misogynistic programming, which also included the infamous segment where Vince McMahon ordered his on-screen former lover, Trish Stratus, to undress, get down on her knees, and "bark like a dog", which was so repugnant that it played a role in derailing Linda McMahon's run for the US senate.

Over time, thanks to the efforts of women like Trish Stratus and Lita, who worked to present more serious women's matches, WWE began to feature more women's wrestling and rebranded its women's division as the "Divas" division. Whilst at least giving women's wrestling a role in the show, it still presented the performers as something less than the men, and the Divas title belt was a pink butterfly, looking more at home in a sticker playset than a wrestling ring. The matches were often short and lacking in story, with the unpleasant "joke" being that they were there to allow fans to take a bathroom break (regrettably, this is still heard: at the G1 Supercard in April 2019, I was queuing for the bathroom before the show began, and the guy behind me got fed up of waiting and said, "screw it, I'll just wait for the women's match").

Nevertheless, the Divas division won fans, and, partly also due to the success of the women's division on WWE's developmental NXT show, the demand for proper women's wrestling grew to a point where the standard script was flipped. After a customary short outing for a women's match on Raw in February 2015, #givedivasachance started trending on Twitter, demanding that WWE give more time and focus to its women's division. WWE revamped its women's division, ditching talk of "Divas", and brought back a Women's Championship for both its Raw and SmackDown shows, along with introducing the company's first ever Women's Tag Team Titles in 2018.

What WWE began branding as the "Divas Revolution" turned into what they now call the "Women's Evolution", which was embodied in event form at WWE's first women's only PPV, *Evolution*, in October 2018. In an October 2018 article in *The Ringer* at the time of the Evolution PPV, Mairead Small Staid made the point that this branding change is significant, and should not be accepted without reflection:

> Among the canniest of WWE's many branding moves over the last three years was the decision to transform the "Divas' Revolution" into a "Women's Evolution." A *revolution* must be fought, demanded, the result of protest and effort and rage, while *evolution* occurs naturally. We don't need to worry about it, the term assures us: Progress will perpetuate itself. But WWE has always been a product of intelligent (or not-so-intelligent, depending on how you feel about the McMahons) design, and survival of the fittest goes only so far, fitted as it must be to the company's monopoly and monarchic ownership.

The term "evolution", Staid suggests, leads us to think that the prominence of women's wrestling was an inevitability; a natural progression of WWE programming over the last few years. It also suggests some necessity of what went before, which – in a sense – aims to justify WWE's prior treatment of women: as part of the evolutionary process, women *had* to be seen as inert valets, then sex objects, then minor performers *before* they could become the major performers they are now; each stage was a necessary part in the natural progression. This is in stark contrast to the term "revolution", which, as Staid points out, suggests agency on the part of those affected, and a prior state of affairs that was *not* OK, and *not* necessary, that was wrong and needed to be corrected. The troubling thing about this terminological shift, then, is that it allows WWE to avoid taking responsibility for the problematic way women have been treated, and gives an excuse for things that are inexcusable. It also prompts the question of whether the internal view towards women has really changed that much, in spite of the external pressures from fans to feature women's wrestling more prominently. It is important to note, too, that the *Evolution* PPV took place five days before another WWE event, *Crown Jewel*, in Saudi Arabia, which was a men-only show by default, as women were not permitted to wrestle by the Saudi government.

We said earlier that it's taken a long time to get here, and now we can ask where *here* really is. There is no denying the significance of the WrestleMania 35 main event, but on a 16-match card (including the pre-show), only three matches were women's matches. The two matches on the main card were title matches, and the one match in the pre-show was a battle royal. According to the *Wrestling Observer Newsletter*'s statistics, only 42 minutes 38 seconds of a seven-plus hour show was devoted to women's matches, with the rest of the time taken by men's matches and other segments. This is a trend that remains frequent in WWE pay-per-views: whilst the profile of women's wrestling has been raised to occasional main event level, there is nowhere near the depth of development of mid-card and lower card women's storylines as there is with the men's roster. Most women's matches on pay-per-view are for a title, whereas the men's division always features non-title-based feuds. This puts a lot of pressure on the women's titles, which tend to be devalued by being traded back and forth a lot more than the men's titles, partly as a result of being a component of the only featured women's matches on a card. The women's tag team titles, which were introduced to much fanfare in 2018, have received scant attention.

There is no doubt that the situation now is probably the best it has ever been for women's wrestling, both in mainstream and independent promotions. The question now is whether this will develop into genuine equality between men and women performers. This is where the WrestleMania main event can have negative effects, in that it provides an easy response for those who wish to sideline women's wrestling: "they headlined WrestleMania, what more do you want?". Whilst it may seem like a culmination (and it was perhaps the culmination of *one storyline*), it should be seen as a beginning: the *start* of women's wrestling being just as significant – if not more so – than men's wrestling. On the evidence of how women's wrestling has been presented since WrestleMania, there is still much work to do to follow up on this beginning.

7. Pushing the Script: Intergender Wrestling

Would a move towards equality be to allow men and women to compete in the same division? This brings us to the controversial case of intergender wrestling: even if we modify the general cultural script to allow both men and women to fight, it seems as though men fighting women is prohibited.

Intergender wrestling in mainstream wrestling companies has never been commonplace, but it has occurred on a number of occasions. In the Hulkamania period, Sherri Martel would frequently mix it up physically with men, who would in turn get physical with her. Jacqueline wrestled a few matches with men in WCW, including a pay-per-view match with Disco Inferno. In the WWF in the late 1990s, the biggest woman star was Chyna, and she not only got physically involved in men's matches, but also frequently wrestled men, including winning the Intercontinental Championship. Lita also wrestled Dean Malenko, Molly Holly won the Hardcore title, and the WWF did intergender mixed-tag team matches, where men and women wrestled each other. At the time, intergender wrestling did not seem to be a big deal, but when WWE moved into PG-rated programming in the 2000s, it all but disappeared. Despite Sexy Star competing with men in *Lucha Underground* from 2014 to 2016, and notably winning the Lucha Underground world title, intergender wrestling was absent from the mainstream for a long time. It has recently resurfaced a few times in WWE, with Ronda Rousey beating up Triple H in their mixed tag team match at WrestleMania 34, and Nia Jax entering the men's Royal Rumble match in 2019. WWE has also offered a "Mixed Match Challenge", which features tag teams of men and women, but this is not true intergender wrestling, as the men only wrestle the men, and the women only wrestle the women. Perhaps the most significant intergender match in a larger company was Tessa Blanchard vs Sami Callihan main-eventing Impact Wrestling's *Slammiversary* show in July 2019.

On the independent circuit, intergender wrestling is much more commonplace, and some promotions even put on shows exclusively featuring intergender matches. It is worth noting too that a lot of women are trained by men, and train with men as they are learning their craft, so it is not uncommon for men and women to wrestle each other behind closed doors. It is one of the more controversial issues in pro wrestling, and we'll take a look at the arguments for and against.

The case for intergender wrestling comes from two separate streams. The first involves equality of opportunity for women more generally in sports, and in other fields. In general, men's sports get more exposure, a higher audience, and the players get more money. Women's sports tend to be less lucrative, and women athletes tend to have a lower profile than their men equivalents. (Compare, for example, the profile and salary that women soccer players have in comparison to men.) However, as noted below, if there is no reason to think that women can't compete at the same level as men, it seems straightforwardly discriminatory to not allow them to do so, particularly as participation in men's sports leads to much higher remuneration. There is no doubt that – despite the strides made in recent years – women's wrestling still has a lower profile than men's, so why shouldn't women be able to compete in the same division as men?

The second stream comes from a slightly different direction. Even if one is doubtful about the first stream, pro wrestling is different from other sports in that it is a work, and, moreover, the audience knows that it is. Pro wrestling is in a unique position in comparison to other sports in that it makes up its own rules, and can present stories, athletes, and matches however it wants to do so. If it wants to present believable intergender wrestling, it can! Indeed, one could argue that pro wrestling would be a great place to present equality between men and women athletes, that could hopefully lead the way for sports to follow.

In terms of arguments against, some object to intergender wrestling because they think it "exposes the business" too much: that it shows too clearly that wrestling is a work, because a woman could never realistically compete with a man in a wrestling match. This seems to me to be completely wrong. Firstly, most fans know it's a work anyway. Secondly, if it's an issue of size, pro wrestling frequently has mismatches between *men* of different sizes – think of Rey Mysterio Jr. vs Kevin Nash, or Finn Balor vs Brock Lesnar – and nobody complains about that as "exposing the business". Men of a size that traditionally would mark them out as cruiserweights, like Daniel Bryan and Rey Mysterio, have also won heavyweight world titles. Thirdly, and most importantly, it just seems straightforwardly prejudicial to say that a woman couldn't realistically compete with a man: some women are stronger, faster, and more athletically gifted than some men, so why wouldn't it be believable that a woman could beat a man in a wrestling match?

More serious objections concern the optics of men and women fighting, when it comes to domestic violence and sexual assault. A man attempting to impose physical dominance over a woman is something that is uncomfortable to watch, and the argument can certainly be made that intergender wrestling struggles when it comes to responsible consideration and presentation of these issues.

In terms of the domestic violence objection, I think there is something to this, particularly if the match is presented in these terms. For example, Tessa Blanchard and Ricochet had what was an incredible wrestling match in Beyond Wrestling in 2017, but the story of the match was the story of an arguing couple (Blanchard and Ricochet were also before this a real-life couple). The match included Ricochet forcibly kissing Blanchard early on (prompting a person in the crowd to yell "that's sexual assault"), and repeatedly saying "sorry honey" before launching attacking moves. Blanchard also tried to goad Ricochet into hitting her by saying "hit me honey", and at one point yelled at him "you should have done the dishes". Judging by the tone of the match, this was intended to be humorous, and that's certainly how the crowd reacted to it, but one wonders whether this is the most responsible way to present intergender wrestling, particularly when that crowd is overwhelmingly made up of men. Domestic violence is not something that should be presented in a humorous way, and one can make the case that this presentation makes way too light of an issue that is very serious.

Another example of a match that pushes the boundaries of taste is Joey Ryan vs Priscilla Kelly in Quintessential Pro Wrestling in 2019. Here the respective genders of the wrestlers played pivotal roles in the story of the match, with each trying to get the other to forcibly touch their genitals, pulling lollipops out of their trunks and attempting to force them in each other's mouths, and the match's key spot where Kelly appeared to vomit on Ryan's penis. Whilst both wrestlers are independently known for their genital-based humor in matches, there was something uneasy about the way it came across in this match, at times being close to mimicking attempts at sexual assault. In a subsequent bout in Ryan's Bar Wrestling promotion, Ryan actually stuck Kelly's head inside his trunks before delivering a piledriver. As in the Blanchard–Ricochet match, it was presented as humorous, but we can ask whether such issues should be made light of in any form of entertainment, not just wrestling.

Intergender wrestling, then, faces challenges that other forms of entertainment do as well, in that it has to be careful how it presents domestic violence and sexual assault. These things should not be played for laughs, even if intergender wrestling provides opportunities to do so.

I don't think that these pitfalls are sufficiently decisive to show that intergender wrestling is never appropriate, however. Moreover, these are just two examples from a very varied field, and I'm not suggesting that all intergender wrestling plays on these issues. A significant problem though is that it is very easy "cheap" heat for the man wrestler to present themselves as a misogynistic pervert, giving the woman wrestler the sympathy of the crowd. But, we can ask whether this is really necessary. For instance, to take a comparison, consider race. Say you have a white man wrestling a black man. It is definitely not OK to have the white man generate heat by using explicitly racist language or gestures. This would generate heat, for sure, but it is tasteless and unnecessary, and not something that would be acceptable. Consider, for example, Roddy Piper's infamous blackface promo before his match against Bad News Brown at WrestleMania VI. Likewise, in intergender wrestling, whilst making sexist or sleazy comments, or indeed acting in these ways, is a way to generate heat, it is not acceptable behavior as these are not things that should merely be used as tools to generate heat on a performer.

In most intergender matches, the man plays the heel. Even in cases where you have a woman who is a heel who the audience want to see get her comeuppance, it is hard for that heat to be sustained throughout an entire match with a man, as opposed to a short, sharp beatdown: if the man babyface prolongs the torment too much, they will lose the audience's sympathy, which will start to transfer to the heel. This dynamic may change if intergender wrestling becomes more commonplace, but, at present, if the man is playing the heel anyway, then they don't really need to resort to uglier forms of heat-gathering. Avoiding this is one way to get around the pitfalls mentioned above.

My sense with intergender wrestling, then, is that it really matters how it is presented. If it is presented as genuine athletic competition which allows women to prove that they are just as good – if not better – than men, then this is OK, if not laudable. If, though, it is framed in such a way as to connect to domestic violence or sexual assault, then this is not OK. Moreover, it seems that these framings are unnecessary: watching the Blanchard–Ricochet match, for example, the wrestling match itself is so good, and so believable on its own as a genuine contest, that the allusions to domestic violence are completely unnecessary to get the match – and the concept – over, and Blanchard has proved this in her other work.

3

Identity: Person vs Gimmick

For the most part, pro wrestlers portray characters. These can be outlandish gimmicks, far from the real person underneath, such as Glenn Jacobs playing the evil dentist Isaac Yankem, DDS, or they can be extensions or amplifications of the real person, such as Stone Cold Steve Austin or The Rock.

Wrestlers are of course not the only people who play characters, but there is often a closeness between a wrestler and their character that is not found in many other places. Actors can get typecast which affects their ability to play different roles, but wrestlers find it especially difficult to reinvent themselves, and distance themselves from characters they've played before. Mark Henry, for example, even though playing a mean, vicious heel later in his career, found it hard to escape the rather daft "Sexual Chocolate" character he played in the late 1990s. Fred Ottman's ill-fated turn as the Shockmaster in WCW effectively ended his career. Fortunately, Becky Lynch managed to leave behind her days as an Irish dancer decked out in sparkly green. Many wrestlers also perform under their real names, which makes the bond between them and their characters even closer. This is happening in TV shows, like *Curb Your Enthusiasm*, but it was happening in wrestling long before this.

In wrestling, unlike in other fields, you often find talk of promotions "burying" talent, particularly if that talent is planning to leave.

For example, in 2019 there was a discussion of whether the WWE was trying to bury the tag team The Revival by making what was a serious act look like fools in an apparent attempt to harm their value and marketability should they leave the company, as they were yet to sign new contracts. This is different from normal acting, as it is hard to bury an actor if they choose to leave a TV show, even if you make their character do silly and degrading things. In wrestling, though, it is different. When a wrestler is on their way out, sometimes a company will do all it can to diminish their value going forward. This is because often there is a tighter connection between the wrestler and their character than there is between an actor and their character.

Thinking about the relationship between the real person and the character leads us to some interesting questions about personal identity, the nature of character, and the nature of a person. For example, What makes a character the same over time? What's the separation between a wrestler and their character? To what extent do we portray characters in our own lives?

1. Where's Razor?

One case of identity that played a significant role in wrestling history occurred in 1996, when Scott Hall and Kevin Nash, who played the characters Razor Ramon and Diesel in the WWF, jumped ship to WCW. When Hall and Nash appeared on WCW TV, the WWF claimed in a lawsuit that they were portraying the WWF-owned characters. This gives us an interesting case to focus on when considering the identity of a character, and their relation to the wrestler who portrays them. We'll mainly look at Scott Hall.

Let's take a particular time – March 1994. Scott Hall is playing

Razor Ramon in the WWF. Now, as is generally the case with character and the people portraying them, the two are not identical. Razor Ramon has Cuban roots, for example, whereas Scott Hall does not. What happens to Razor Ramon *the character* is not happening to Scott Hall *the person*. For example, Razor Ramon is feuding with Shawn Michaels, but *Scott Hall* is not feuding with Shawn Michaels, nor is he feuding with the person playing that Shawn Michaels character, Michael Hickenbottom (indeed, the two are becoming close friends). At this point, it is fairly clear that the person and the character can be separated.

Now let's fast-forward to May 1996. Scott Hall has left the WWF for WCW. Though occasionally reported this way at the time, "Razor Ramon" *cannot* have left the WWF for WCW, as Razor Ramon is a WWF-owned character. What, then, happens to the character Razor Ramon: does the character continue to exist? Is this the end of the character, as its portrayer is no longer around? Let's see what happened.

Hall shows up on WCW Monday Nitro, and cuts a promo which suggests that he is an invading "outsider". While he doesn't state his name, he does say that "you people know who I am", which seemingly makes reference to his run in the WWF as Razor Ramon. He also speaks with a faux-Cuban accent, has his hair styled in the same way as he did in the WWF, and sports a toothpick in his mouth, just as Razor Ramon did. However, as the WWF owns the copyright for the character Razor Ramon, he cannot be acknowledged on WCW TV *as* Razor Ramon. Indeed, it seems as though it would be *impossible* for him to play Razor Ramon on WCW TV, as that character is only authorized to appear on WWF shows.

Unsurprisingly, the WWF objected to Hall's actions on Nitro, and filed a lawsuit for copyright infringement: despite WCW not using the name "Razor Ramon", the WWF alleged that they were presenting a character that was *sufficiently similar*, thus creating confusion in the minds of the audience as to whether or not *Razor Ramon* (not Scott Hall) was appearing on WCW TV.

Here the philosophy of character is interesting: the WWF is not claiming that Hall *is* portraying Razor Ramon, as – due to their owning the character – this would strictly speaking be impossible unless *they* authorized the performance. What they are objecting to is the portrayal of a similar character that is not sufficiently acknowledged to be distinct from the WWF-owned character, and hence the apparent attempt to trick the audience into thinking that they are seeing Razor Ramon on WCW TV, which is, strictly speaking, impossible without the WWF's authorization.

What makes this even more interesting is that in September 1996, the WWF aimed to make a splash by advertising the "return" of Razor Ramon to the WWF. At first glance, this led some to believe that *Scott Hall* would be returning to the WWF, which would have been a major coup for the WWF given Hall's success in WCW at the time. It became apparent, though, as soon as "Razor Ramon" was reintroduced, that Scott Hall had not returned, but instead another wrestler – Rick Bognar – was portraying the Razor Ramon character. As the WWF owned the Razor Ramon character, this was something they were free to do (and it helped bolster their copyright infringement case against WCW).

This move was not received well by fans. Even though, strictly speaking, this *was* Razor Ramon – the character – the fact that Razor was played by a different wrestler was a significant problem in terms of the fans accepting this character. In wrestling lore, this character is known as "Fake Razor", as opposed to the genuine Razor Ramon. This is interesting as, as noted before, there was a difference between the original portrayer of the character, Scott Hall, and the

Razor Ramon character. In legal terms at least, the WWF, not Scott Hall, had dominion over the Razor Ramon character. However, in the fans' eyes, the character was much more closely associated with the original performer, and the attempt to introduce the character with a different portrayer was soundly rejected. As Jim Cornette put it in a WhatCulture Q&A, "The guy is what makes the gimmick. The gimmick don't make the guy".

We can ask the question: *where* was Razor Ramon in October 1996? Was he in the WWF, where the Razor Ramon character was portrayed by Rick Bognar, or was he in WCW, where Scott Hall now worked? The WWF would have categorically said that Razor Ramon was in the WWF, and that there was an imposter in WCW, tricking fans into thinking that Razor was there instead. The fans, though, seemed to take the opposing view: the WWF's Razor was the imposter, the "fake", and the real Razor was now in WCW. We have two different views about character identity here: the first has it that those who own the copyright have complete control over the character, and what they say goes. The second has it that at least some control lies in the hands of the consumers – or fans – who are the primary audience for the character, and that what they decide on in regard to a character carries more weight than the copyright holder.

This conflict shows an interesting feature of public entities. In a sense, the character Razor Ramon is an institutional entity: a copyrighted character, owned by a corporation. In these terms, there isn't a question of where Razor Ramon is in October 1996: he is in the WWF, being portrayed by Rick Bognar. The WWF owns the character, and the rights to it, so wherever they say it is, it is. The lack of acceptance of this truth by fans and the wider wrestling community, though, suggests that this is not decisive: there can be an evolution of the nature of an entity that transcends its origin, and changes its nature from what it was originally intended to be. Whilst an institution has *some* control over the entities it creates, the broader public has a degree of control too over whether or not they *accept* the legitimacy of the institution and its creation.

Consider marriage, for example. This is an institutional entity, and the nature of marriage – for a long time – involved the union of a man and a woman. This was the institutional definition of marriage, and same-sex partnerships, no matter how devoted and long-lasting, just *were not marriage*. However, over time, due to evolution in the way the public viewed it, the nature of marriage *as an entity* was changed when same-sex marriage became legal. The institutions that created marriage did not have full control over the nature of marriage due to the way marriage was perceived by the public. The refusal to accept that marriage could only be between a man and a woman led to a change in what marriage is.

So, institutional entities are also *public* entities, and public opinion retains some control over the nature of those entities. Despite the WWF having legal ownership over the character Razor Ramon, what the case of the "fake" Razor showed was that they didn't really own the character in all respects. Fans took part ownership of the character by refusing to accept the change that was forced upon them: *this* is not *our* Razor!

This does not always happen. For example, the masked WWE character Sin Cara was initially portrayed by Luis Urive in 2011. In 2013, however, the character began being portrayed by Jorge Arias. Even though many fans knew there was a new wrestler under the mask, there was not the rejection of the new wrestler in the way that there had been with Razor Ramon. The same can be said for Doink the Clown, another masked character – originally played by Matt Borne – who was also played by a number of other wrestlers. The mask could play a big role in these cases, as the characters were able to be presented more-or-less the same way visually, or maybe fans were not so concerned as there wasn't such a blatant attempt to ignore the realities of the situations.

A third answer to the question of where Razor Ramon was in October 1996 is that Razor was nowhere; that, after Scott Hall parted ways with the WWF, Razor Ramon the character ceased to exist. On this view, *both* the WWF's Razor and WCW's Scott Hall are imposters, as there is no Razor Ramon any more. This view suggests that there is an intimate connection between a character and the person who plays them, and if those two part ways, then the character is no more. Notice, though, that this flies in the face of some of the things we said earlier about the *distinction* between a character and the person who plays them. The idea here seems to be that the character Razor Ramon is such that the character must *necessarily* be portrayed by Scott Hall. Whilst this doesn't imply that Razor Ramon and Scott Hall are *identical*, it does place a condition on the existence of the character: that it must be portrayed by Scott Hall, or else it does not exist.

Despite flirting with the idea of calling Hall "The Bad Guy", which was also a moniker associated with Razor Ramon in the WWF, WCW eventually decided to just refer to him by his real name, Scott Hall. This was in line with their general move toward more reality-based storylines and characters, and calling Hall by his given name as opposed to a gimmick name was a bold statement. Something which would previously have marked a wrestler out as a jobber was now a sign that they were a top guy.

Hall went on to have a storied, yet troubled, career in WCW, and made a brief return to the WWF in 2002 a year or so after the WWF had bought WCW. He returned *as* Scott Hall, in his WCW character as part of the nWo. Controversially, much of Scott Hall's real-life struggles with alcohol and substance abuse were brought into his storylines, both in WCW and the WWF, blurring the lines between the character Scott Hall, and the real person.

But what happened to Razor Ramon? The "fake" Razor played by Rick Bognar in the WWF disappeared in January 1997, never to be seen again. But, there is a further twist to the story. Curiously, Razor Ramon – not Scott Hall – was inducted into the WWE Hall of Fame in 2014. It was Scott Hall *as* Razor Ramon who was inducted, but not Scott Hall himself, rather the character he portrayed for a short portion of his career in the WWF in the mid-1990s. This was in contrast to Kevin Nash, who was inducted *as Kevin Nash*, not Diesel.

So, *who* was inducted into the Hall of Fame? WWE has a vested interest in inducting their own creation – the character Razor Ramon – rather than something that had been made successful by their then competitors. But, it is undeniable that Hall's influence on the wrestling business, and his legacy as a wrestler, was made by his run *as Scott Hall* in WCW, in particular as a founding member of the nWo.

Ironically, when you look at the WWE bio page for Razor Ramon on wwe.com, the page lists not only features of Razor's WWF run in the mid-1990s, but also aspects of Scott Hall's career in general, including his pre-WWF run in WCW as the Diamond Studd, and his post-WWF run in WCW as Scott Hall. By listing these activities and achievements as those of "Razor Ramon", are WWE now suggesting that Hall *was* in fact Razor Ramon all this time?

Looking at the text on his WWE bio, this seems to be exactly what they are suggesting:

With his WWE contract status unknown to the public, Razor appeared unannounced on WCW Monday Nitro on May 27, 1996 . . .

> WCW stars Sting, Lex Luger and "Macho Man" Randy Savage joined forces to battle Razor – who was now competing under his given name of Scott Hall – and Nash at Bash at the Beach. (wwe.com/superstars/razor-ramon)

The suggestion here is that it *was* Razor Ramon who went to WCW after all! Of course, when this profile was posted, WWE owned WCW, so they were less concerned about issues like copyright infringement, but it does seem inconsistent with what they claimed at the time in 1996. It also renders incomprehensible the claim that Rick Bognar played Razor Ramon, as Razor Ramon is now explicitly identified with Scott Hall! So, in 1996 the WWF made significant claims that distinguished Scott Hall from Razor Ramon, but now in 2019 WWE states that they are (and seemingly always have been) one and the same. Is this WWE bowing to fan pressure, and admitting that they were wrong to present Rick Bognar as Razor Ramon? Or, more cynically, is this WWE taking ownership of Scott Hall's achievements by ensuring that he remains branded as a WWE character?

2. Working Yourself into a Shoot

What we saw with Razor was a case of how to characterize identity from the outside: how we, as fans, or as corporations, determine what character someone is playing. But what about identity from the inside? What happens when wrestlers *identify themselves* too closely with their characters on TV?

Acting as your character all the time was a central feature of the wrestling business for a long time. To keep kayfabe, many wrestlers had to keep in character all the time, and the practice was much like method acting. They couldn't let the fans see the person behind the character, which also meant that they couldn't travel with, or be seen in public with, people they were feuding with. When Hacksaw Jim Duggan and the Iron Sheik were arrested for drug possession after a traffic stop in 1987, the WWF's main problem with them was not the drugs, but that they were traveling together when in a blood feud. They were both fired. This evidently takes a toll on personal relationships, both friendships between wrestlers, and their relationships with their families when they were required to be in character most of the time. Today, even though this aspect of kayfabe is no longer expected, social media provides a peculiar realm for the lines between wrestling character and real person to be blurred. Many pro wrestlers have a Twitter account where they post as both the "real person", and as their character, furthering storylines. Many times it's hard to tell the difference between the two, both for us observing, and for them posting.

Matters are complicated further by the fact that real aspects of a person's life are sometimes incorporated into their wrestling character. Think of the on-screen relationship between Macho Man Randy Savage and Elizabeth, which was heavily influenced by the fact that – for a time – they were married in real life. What were fans witnessing when, at SummerSlam 1991, Savage and Elizabeth were "married" on screen (they had been married in real life since 1984)? Real affection? Performed affection? Both? A similar scenario was played out in WWE in 2019 between Becky Lynch and Seth Rollins, and WWE features a number of real-life couples together on screen in character. There are also the multiple relationships in the McMahon family that have been dramatized in seemingly endless WWE storylines, and the real-life father–son, brother–brother relationships in the Rhodes/Runnels family between Dusty, Dustin, and Cody.

In these cases, pre-existing relationships are incorporated into a character and their storyline, an aspect of pro wrestling that is pretty unique, especially when compared to conventional actors in TV shows. The line between the real person and the character becomes blurred, as there are aspects of the character that are also true of the person performing. Sometimes these incorporations make for compelling viewing, as they tread that line between reality and performance so closely that it's hard to tell what's real and what's not, which creates the intrigue we talked about earlier in the book. Other times, they can cut a bit too close to the bone and be a bit tasteless, such as when a person's real problems with alcohol or drug addiction are made into a TV storyline, as happened with Scott Hall. Or, indeed, when real-life bereavements are involved, such as the Big Boss Man's infamous crashing of the Big Show's father's "funeral", driving off towing the coffin down the street, or the use of the death of Natalya's father during her feud with Ruby Riott.

Things can go the other way too, in that someone starts off very distinct from their character, but ends up becoming the character after an extended period of playing them. Becoming your character is sometimes called working yourself into a shoot, as your working persona – your character – becomes one and the same as your real, or "shoot", persona. Some wrestlers *become* their gimmicks (although, perhaps for copyright reasons!). For example, Jim Hellwig, who played the Ultimate Warrior in the WWF in the late 1980s/early 1990s, changed his legal name to "Warrior"; and Ryan Reeves, who played Ryback in WWE in the 2010s, changed his legal name to "Ryback Reeves".

It is often those who perform under their real names – or names close enough to them – though, where the line becomes more and more blurred. Ric Flair (born "Richard Fliehr"), is one example of a wrestler who lived his "stylin', profilin', limousine riding, jet flying, kiss-stealing, wheelin'n'dealin' son of a gun!" "nature boy" (or "Naitch", for short) gimmick, to the point where he was never *not* playing his wrestling persona. As Shawn Michaels puts it in the 2017 ESPN 30 for 30 documentary, *Nature Boy*:

> Ric doesn't love Richard Fliehr. I don't know that he's ever taken the time to get to know him or to find out who in the world he is. He only knows who he is through the image and gimmick of Ric Flair.

Ric Flair himself follows up on this in the same documentary:

> Richard Fliehr was just someone who made it through one year of college. After that it was the Naitch.

Another example, which connects back to earlier discussions, is Bret Hart in 1997. Paul Jay's 1998 documentary *Hitman Hart: Wrestling with Shadows* gives us some key insights into how Bret viewed himself and his character during this time. One scene shows Bret, by now well into his anti-American persona, saying the following on WWF Raw:

> If you were going to give the United States of America an enema, you'd stick the hose right here in Pittsburgh, Pennsylvania. (WWF Raw is War, 7/28/97, *WWE Network*)

Hart shortly after reflects on what he said:

> That wasn't my idea to say that. I'm urged – not forced – but I'm urged to say this, to really get 'em going. And in retrospect, now looking back I think it was a mistake to say that. *That's not me,*

I wouldn't have said that, I don't personally think that. If I was going to stick the hose in the United States, I certainly wouldn't look at Pittsburgh. (*Hitman Hart: Wrestling with Shadows*)

Look at the italicized words above. Bret is reflecting on what he said as if what he says in the ring ought to be a reflection of what *he himself* really thinks. But, in wrestling, there is no expectation of this: there is supposed to be a clear distinction between a person's wrestling persona and them in real life. For Hart, here, the line between the real person and the character has become blurred in his mind.

This is one of the factors that leads to the Montreal Screwjob. Bret takes things *personally*, in that what happens to his character is something that he perceives as happening *to him*. Bret *has* to be the hero in Canada, and that's why he can't lose the title to Shawn in Montreal. Note that there's a difference between protecting one's character, and one's character's ability to draw (e.g. as Hulk Hogan was often seen to do), and seeing oneself *as* one's character, and protecting one's character the way one would protect oneself.

Notably, after the Screwjob, at the end of the documentary, Bret seems to suggest a separation between himself and the character, perhaps because of the damage done:

It's almost a fitting end to the Hitman character, cos he never sold out, and he never lost his integrity. Bret Hart came home, he's fine. What they did is they murdered this Hitman character. (*Hitman Hart: Wrestling with Shadows*)

Hart's subsequent time in WCW is mainly viewed as a failure, in part because of WCW's creative ideas, but also because Bret had fallen out of love with wrestling, and didn't care about his character development they way he used to. The death of his character, as he puts it, was also a death of something key about him. It's not clear that Bret Hart really *was* fine after this.

A complaint sometimes made about Hart is that he took himself too seriously, or "became a mark for himself". He began to see wrestling as something real, that was happening to him, as opposed to showbusiness, that involved his character. Whilst this is presented as a criticism, it's also one of the things that allowed Hart to excel in his chosen profession. For many of us, if we care about what we do, and invest ourselves in it, we do better than we otherwise would do. It is nice to be able to separate oneself from one's work, but it is not always possible to do so in a way that allows you to succeed. Indeed, Steve Austin, who became perhaps the biggest wrestling star ever, has repeatedly said that during his time of success, it was a shoot to him, and he took his character just as seriously as Hart did – if not more so.

This allows us to reflect on what this all tells us about our own lives. With wrestlers, the distinction between the people and their working characters, or "gimmicks", is usually obvious, though sometimes it is not. It's harder for us to discern for ourselves, or our friends or family members, what the difference is between ourselves and our working personas. When we say to someone, "don't take this personally", or "it's not personal, it's just business", or "don't take yourself too seriously", we are effectively asking people to separate their business, or work, persona from themselves as they really are. Sometimes this is hard to do if what you're working on is something you care deeply about. Sometimes then there is no difference for you between yourself and your working aspirations.

3. The *Real* Me?

We all present different faces to the world at different times. Which of those is the real one? All of them? None of them? Do we ever really know? As Bret Hart himself puts it in his book, *Hitman*:

> Later on in life I was one guy on the road, another at home and yet another in the ring. Which one is truly me? They all are. (Hart 2007: 4)

This search for the *real me* is one that preoccupies many people, but is there anything really there beyond the various faces we present to the world? The idea that there is no real, fundamental, self that essentially marks who a person is is most famously expressed in philosophy by the Scottish Enlightenment philosopher David Hume, who says in his *Treatise of Human Nature*:

> The mind is a kind of theatre, where several perceptions successively make their appearance; pass, repass, glide away, and mingle in an infinite variety of postures and situations. (Hume, *Treatise* I:IV: vi)

Hume's idea was that, whenever we try to get a sense of our selves, we can only ever get a sense of ourselves *at a particular moment*, complete with all the thoughts, feelings, and sensations of that moment. Given that these change from moment to moment, our sense of our selves changes with it, and what we experience in our lives is a succession of different selves, as opposed to one constant self. We can apply this thought to what Bret Hart says above, in that, whenever Bret tries to get a sense of *who he really is*, he can only ever catch himself at one moment, in one mode, whether it be on the road, at home, or in the ring. There is no *real* Bret Hart over and above all of these incarnations; the succession of different guys are all the real Bret Harts.

Compare this also to Mick Foley's "three faces of Foley": Cactus Jack, Mankind, and Dude Love. These three characters that Foley has portrayed over the years are occasionally presented as representing different sides to Foley's character. When Mick Foley wrestles *as Mick Foley*, he incorporates aspects of each of these characters into his performance, further developing the idea that they are components of his own character. Again, if we were to ask which of them is the *real* Mick Foley, the answer would probably be that none are. And yet, in a way, all of them are, at least if we are talking about Foley's wrestling persona.

Hume's ideas led some philosophers, such as Derek Parfit, to suggest that, when we think of the life of a person, we don't think of one continuous life of one continuous self, but rather a succession of selves over the course of time. A person when they are 8 years old is very different from when they are 18, 28, or 80, and, according to Parfit, we should treat these stages *as different people*, who are suitably connected to make them care significantly about the others' well-being and interests.

What goes for real people goes for wrestling characters too. Many characters undergo substantial changes through the course of a career, to the point where it is hard to say that there is *one* character that has persisted through all this time. Take Chris Jericho, for example, who has gone through a number of transformations *as Chris Jericho* throughout his career. We have the "Lionheart" Chris Jericho, the cocky "man of 1004 holds" Chris Jericho, Y2J Chris Jericho, the solemn, serious, suit-wearing Chris Jericho, the flashing jacket Chris Jericho, the scarf-wearing "List" Chris Jericho, the "Alpha" Chris

Jericho, the deranged clown Chris Jericho, the "painmaker" Chris Jericho, and the bruising "evil" Chris Jericho. This is a case where it really does seem as though we have a succession of different characters that are all connected, as opposed to one, single, continuous character that merely takes different forms.

Pro wrestling characters can shift dramatically over time, to the point where they look different, and act differently at different times. They can also be good guys at one time and bad guys at another, friends with a character at one time and enemies later. These shifts are often dramatic, and amplified, but they do give us an exaggerated vision of what happens to us during our own lives. We change the way we look, we change the way we act, and wouldn't do now some things that we did when we were younger. We go through times where we are more bad than good, and times when we are more good than bad. Our relationships with family and friends fluctuate, to the point where, sometimes, we are not speaking to a person who at other times is our closest friend. And, somehow, we try to knit all these stages together into a somewhat coherent narrative, which is our life.

4

Morality: Babyface vs Heel

What is it to be a good person? What about a bad person? What can make a good person turn bad? These are moral questions at the foundation of pro wrestling storylines. Pro wrestling storylines typically take the form of a hero (the "babyface") taking on a villain (the "heel"). Traditionally, babyfaces and heels would exhibit very specific characteristics. The babyface would be earnest, honest, and brave, and the heel would be deceptive, a cheat, and a coward. Each match was then set up as effectively a battle of good vs evil, of virtue against vice, with themes of justice, retribution, and redemption prominent.

However, in the late 1990s, the structure of pro wrestling storylines and characters changed, disrupting this traditional picture of virtue and vice. The rise of the New World Order in WCW and Stone Cold Steve Austin in the WWF presented new heroes to the audience that did not display many of the traditional virtues, and, indeed, exhibited many vices. In modern pro wrestling, lines are increasingly blurred between heroes and villains, and it is harder to find clear examples of characters that fit the traditional babyface and heel roles. In this chapter we will examine what this tells us about morality, and our attitudes toward it.

1. The Classic View

Pro wrestling characters and storylines have historically been drawn in terms of the classic struggle between good and evil. Your classic American pro wrestling match pits a babyface against a heel, with the crowd cheering for the babyface, and booing the heel. There are very specific markers of each type of character, which allow the audience to work out which is which. Babyfaces typically wear bright colors (though nothing too ostentatious), smile, are enthusiastic, and high five the crowd as they make their way to the ring. Heels typically wear somber colors, are surly and scowl at the audience, show little signs of enthusiasm, and insult the crowd. Alternatively, heels can be too over-the-top in their flamboyance, displaying arrogance, and are overly preening or concerned with their appearance. This difference between kinds of heels is explicitly captured in Mexican Lucha Libre wrestling by the use of different terms for different kinds of heels. "Rudos" are the mean heels, and "exoticos" are the more preening, flamboyant heels.

On the mic, the babyface will express earnestness and desire for fair competition, and a wholesome desire to triumph the right way. They will be respectful to the crowd, and not overly insulting to their opponent. Heels, on the other hand, will show little respect to anyone, particularly the crowd, and will attempt to get what they want through whatever nefarious means are available. In the ring, the babyface will show great energy and courage, and attempt to win through fair means. They won't cheat, use weapons, or intimidate the referee. Heels will do the opposite. They will show cowardice by begging off when their opponent is on the attack, they will use dirty tactics to try to win, and will not shy away from intimidating the referee or other officials.

We can list the typical virtues of babyfaces, and vices of heels, as follows:

- Babyface virtues: courage, enthusiasm, fairness, justice, respect, protecting the weak.
- Heel vices: cowardice, disinterest, arrogance, cheating, disrespect, preying upon the weak.

In this classic conception, pro wrestling storylines portray a very familiar battle between good and evil: there are good people, who exhibit a specific set of virtues, and bad people, who exhibit a specific set of vices. The ring is the arena for this battle between good and evil, and the crowd are desperate for good to prevail. Sometimes it does, and sometimes it doesn't, just as in many other kinds of dramatic performance.

Even in this classic conception, it is not the case that each character is *intrinsically* good or evil. Over the course of the years, many characters move from being good to being evil, and vice versa. Babyface characters can "turn heel", and abandon all that made them good, including rejecting the adulation of their fans. Heels can "turn babyface", and redeem themselves in the eyes of the fans by doing good acts unexpectedly. Again, this is something not uncommon in other forms of extended dramatic performance. Think about the character of Anakin Skywalker in the Star Wars movies. He starts as a babyface, undergoes a gradual heel turn, then stays heel for a long time as Darth Vader, before an eventual babyface turn at the end of *Return of the Jedi*, when he saves Luke Skywalker from the Emperor. Most pro wrestlers will undergo similar transformations throughout the course of their careers, and it is very rare (if not unheard of) for a wrestler to have a career where they are just a heel, or just a babyface.

2. Virtues and Vices

The morality of American pro wrestling is very much focused on character: virtues and vices. What we are interested in as fans is the character of the wrestlers involved, and the things they are disposed to do as a result of that character. If they cheat, we boo them; if they play fair, we cheer them. When it comes to philosophical views about morality, this smacks of Aristotle's influential approach to ethics, often called "virtue ethics". Aristotle held that a person's goal should be to be virtuous, and gave a very detailed account of the various virtues and vices that a person could have. For Aristotle, virtue is the mean between two corresponding vices, and, to be virtuous, one needs to practice the difficult art of finding the correct balance. Table 1 shows the full list from Book II of Aristotle's *Nicomachean Ethics*.

If you look down the list of virtues (in the "Mean" column), you will find that most (if not all) of these are exhibited by classic babyfaces. Take a straightforward "white meat" babyface: John Cena, since 2010 in WWE. Cena is presented as a classic "never-say-die" good guy, who is a wholesome role model for younger viewers. If we look at Cena's character traits in relation to Aristotle's list, in Table 2, we find that he is all virtue, and no vices.

Indeed, this is the formula used for most babyfaces in the classic mold, such as Hulk Hogan in the 1980s, Sting in the early 1990s, Bret Hart in the mid-1990s, and Bayley in the late 2010s. These characters, maybe partly because of their intended appeal to children, were not permitted any character flaws.

When we consider heels, things are a little more interesting, as, though there is only one way to be virtuous, there are two different ways to exhibit vices, either in terms of deficiency or excess, and different kinds of heels exhibit vices in different ways. One of the most

Table 1. Aristotle on the Virtues

Sphere of Action or Feeling	Excess	Mean	Deficiency
Fear and Confidence	Rashness	Courage	Cowardice
Pleasure and Pain	Licentiousness/ Self-indulgence	Temperance	Insensibility
Getting and Spending (minor)	Prodigality	Liberality	Illiberality/Meanness
Getting and Spending (major)	Vulgarity/ Tastelessness	Magnificence	Pettiness/Stinginess
Honor and Dishonor (major)	Vanity	Magnanimity	Pusillanimity
Honor and Dishonor (minor)	Ambition/Empty vanity	Proper ambition/Pride	Unambitiousness/ Undue humility
Anger	Irascibility	Patience/Good temper	Lack of spirit/ Unirascibility
Self-expression	Boastfulness	Truthfulness	Understatement/Mock modesty
Conversation	Buffoonery	Wittiness	Boorishness
Social Conduct	Obsequiousness	Friendliness	Cantankerousness
Shame	Shyness	Modesty	Shamelessness
Indignation	Envy	Righteous indignation	Malicious enjoyment/ Spitefulness

legendary heels was Ric Flair in the 1980s. As the travelling National Wrestling Alliance (NWA) champion, Flair would travel the country defending his title in different territories against the local favorites. Flair was an extravagant character: "The Stylin', profilin', limousine riding, jet flying, kiss-stealing, wheelin'n'dealin' son of a gun!", who lived his gimmick. His genius as a heel was to make himself look beatable in his matches against the local heroes, making the crowd believe they could beat him, before he stole a victory. Flair used all the various nefarious means available to him to win his matches, and displayed very few – if any – of the classical virtues. Indeed, if we plot Flair's character traits as in Table 3, we find that he doesn't exhibit any.

Table 2. John Cena from 2010 onwards

Sphere of Action or Feeling	Excess	Mean	Deficiency
Fear and Confidence	Rashness	**Courage**	Cowardice
Pleasure and Pain	Licentiousness/ Self-indulgence	**Temperance**	Insensibility
Getting and Spending (minor)	Prodigality	**Liberality**	Illiberality/Meanness
Getting and Spending (major)	Vulgarity/ Tastelessness	**Magnificence**	Pettiness/Stinginess
Honor and Dishonor (major)	Vanity	**Magnanimity**	Pusillanimity
Honor and Dishonor (minor)	Ambition/Empty vanity	**Proper ambition/ Pride**	Unambitiousness/ Undue humility
Anger	Irascibility	**Patience/Good temper**	Lack of spirit/ Unirascibility
Self-expression	Boastfulness	**Truthfulness**	Understatement/Mock modesty
Conversation	Buffoonery	**Wittiness**	Boorishness
Social Conduct	Obsequiousness	**Friendliness**	Cantankerousness
Shame	Shyness	**Modesty**	Shamelessness
Indignation	Envy	**Righteous indignation**	Malicious enjoyment/ Spitefulness

It is also worth noting that some heels had a "signature" vice, which was a key part of their character, and often drove the storylines they were involved in. In many cases, this vice ultimately led to the heel's downfall, telling a cautionary tale to the audience. For example, the "Million Dollar Man" Ted DiBiase was presented as a greedy, wealth-obsessed individual, and this became key in the story of his feud with Jake "the Snake" Roberts, culminating in a match at WrestleMania VI. DiBiase's greed was the main focus of Jake's promo before the match, which has gone down as one of the greatest promos of all time:

Well, well. The Million Dollar Man, Ted DiBiase. Here we are at WrestleMania, and it's the biggest match of your career.

Table 3. Ric Flair in the 1980s

Sphere of Action or Feeling	Excess	Mean	Deficiency
Fear and Confidence	Rashness	Courage	**Cowardice**
Pleasure and Pain	**Licentiousness/ Self-indulgence**	Temperance	Insensibility
Getting and Spending (minor)	**Prodigality**	Liberality	Illiberality/Meanness
Getting and Spending (major)	**Vulgarity/ Tastelessness**	Magnificence	Pettiness/Stinginess
Honor and Dishonor (major)	**Vanity**	Magnanimity	Pusillanimity
Honor and Dishonor (minor)	**Ambition/Empty vanity**	Proper ambition/Pride	Unambitiousness/ Undue humility
Anger	**Irascibility**	Patience/Good temper	Lack of spirit/ Unirascibility
Self-expression	**Boastfulness**	Truthfulness	Understatement/Mock modesty
Conversation	**Buffoonery**	Wittiness	Boorishness
Social Conduct	Obsequiousness	Friendliness	**Cantankerousness**
Shame	Shyness	Modesty	**Shamelessness**
Indignation	Envy	Righteous indignation	**Malicious enjoyment/ Spitefulness**

Why? Because everything you stand for is on the line, namely, the Million Dollar Belt. Oh yeah, you see it can be yours once again. All you have to do is go through Damien, and me. But you see, Damien and I don't forget, we remember all the times you made people grovel for your money. These were people far less fortunate than you, people who could use your money for essentials, and what did you do? You made fun of them. You humbled them and you humiliated them. Well, now it's my turn. I'm going to make you beg, DiBiase, you are going to get down on your hands and knees. This time, you'll be the one that's humbled. This time, you'll be the one that's humiliated, and this time, you will be the one that grovels for the money. And how appropriate, that the money you grovel for is your very own. A victim of your own greed, wallowing in the muck of avarice. (WWF WrestleMania VI, *WWE Network*)

For other heels, different vices were more prominent. Viciousness and spitefulness, for example, such as in Eddie Guerrero's obsessive pursuit of Rey Mysterio Jr.'s mask in WCW in 1997, or boastfulness in Ronda Rousey's feud with Becky Lynch in 2019. The moral message is the same, though: indulgence in vice, whilst it may lead to short-term gains, ultimately leads to your downfall, as it did for Eddie, who lost his cruiserweight title to Rey as a result, and to Rousey, whose boastfulness in thinking that, as a former UFC Champion, she could beat any wrestler, lost her title to Lynch when pinned with a wrestling move. Justice is thus a key aspect of pro wrestling storylines: even if the heel has some success, they will be brought down by the babyface eventually. Good must prevail!

3. Turns

Some of the more dramatic moments in wrestling are points where characters tease turning from babyface to heel, or vice versa. For example, the narrative structure of Bret Hart and Roddy Piper's Intercontinental Championship match at WWF WrestleMania VIII was built around the recently redeemed Piper's temptations to go to the dark side and use a weapon against a fallen Hart. Piper's hesitation as he held the ring bell in his hand, and the crowd's desperate pleading with him not to use it, was the most dramatic moment of the match, and Piper's subsequent refusal to use the ring bell was presented as a large part of his loss in the match, and the loss of his title.

Moments where characters *do* change from babyface to heel, or vice versa, are amongst the most memorable in the history of the genre. Hulk Hogan's heel turn at WCW Bash at the Beach '96, for example, is often discussed as the most significant and shocking moment in contemporary American pro wrestling. Other shock turns include The Rock's heel turn at WWF Survivor Series '98, and Stone Cold Steve Austin's heel turn at WrestleMania 17. When done well, these are very interesting moments from a character point of view, as they show a character at breaking point; at a point where what has previously worked for them no longer does, and they are forced into a change, for better or for worse.

Hogan's turn was probably the most shocking, both from a kayfabe, storyline perspective, and from a real-life business perspective. Hogan, of course, had been the number one babyface in pro wrestling for around 10 years, in both the WWF and WCW. The success of the WWF in the late 1980s/early 1990s had been built around Hogan, including the concept of the biggest wrestling event every year, WrestleMania. Hogan was easily the most recognizable face in wrestling, and had a good degree of mainstream recognition. His appeal to kids was legendary, as was his ability to sell red-and-yellow merchandise spreading Hulkamania worldwide to all the little Hulkamaniacs. In 1994, after spending some time away from wrestling filming movies and TV shows, Hogan signed a massive deal with WCW to return to wrestling. He immediately unseated the WCW champion, Ric Flair, and went on to more-or-less continue the same character work and storylines that had brought him success in the late 1980s.

In 1996, though, this was getting a little stale, and fans were starting to tire of the classic Hogan act. Eric Bischoff noticed this, and pitched Hogan the idea of joining the invading Scott Hall and Kevin Nash, and becoming the mysterious "third man" in the New World

Order (nWo) storyline. Hogan was unsure, as this was a big risk for his character. Not only would it overturn the classic good guy he had been for so long, but it could have major financial implications: he would be giving up all the money from the merchandise so eagerly snapped up by the little Hulkamaniacs. It was also a risk for WCW, who had brought Hogan in precisely because of who he *was*: the biggest star in wrestling, and all that that entailed. Hogan was apparently unsure about whether to go through with the heel turn right up until it happened.

On the night in question – Bash at the Beach, 1996 – the main event saw Hall and Nash take on WCW heroes Sting, Randy Savage, and Lex Luger. It was billed as a 3-on-3 tag match, but Hall and Nash showed up without their partner, who they promised would show up when he was ready. Hall and Nash were dominating the match, when out came Hulk Hogan, surely to save the WCW stars! Instead, Hogan gave Savage his leg drop finisher, and then celebrated with Hall and Nash. In an interview afterwards with "Mean" Gene Okerland, Hogan disparaged WCW and the fans, hailing the "New World Order" of wrestling. The shocked crowd booed Hogan out the building, and threw all sorts of trash in the ring. The heel heat generated by this move was astronomical, and it led to the best business WCW ever did (and, ironically, the best-selling merchandise – the nWo T-shirt).

4. The Classic View Disrupted

Hogan's heel turn was during a time of general overhaul of the traditional American moral pro wrestling set up. The classic formula of babyfaces and heels, along with their associated roles, was dramatically disrupted in the late 1990s. Fans had grown tired of the classic formula, and the wrestling business was suffering as a result, with attendance and pay-per-view buys dropping significantly from the heyday of the late 1980s.

The more reality-focused nWo storyline in WCW turned things around. The nWo was presented as an invading band of wrestlers, who beat people up with baseball bats, attacked at random (including Kevin Nash throwing Rey Mysterio Jr. like a lawn dart into the side of a trailer), and even assaulted members of the broadcast team. In contrast to the more cartoonish characters usually seen in wrestling, they were presented as more realistic characters, in some cases using their real names, as with Scott Hall and Kevin Nash. They were also – unlike many other wrestlers – *cool*, and their anti-establishment antics resonated with the audience.

In the WWF, the late 1990s marked a remarkable rise for the character of Stone Cold Steve Austin. Originally presented as a vicious and dastardly heel, Austin's character of a beer-swilling, no-nonsense, tough guy began to resonate with the audience. An unusual change was occurring where traditional babyfaces (like Rocky Maivia) were being booed, and heels, like Steve Austin, were being cheered. Some people thought of this as the American audience "turning heel", as would be exploited by Bret Hart's heel turn in the spring/summer of 1997.

Take Austin's defining moment in the early part of his rise to stardom: his 1996 King of the Ring tournament win, and the subsequent promo he cut after winning. In the final of the tournament, he battered a WWF legend, Jake "the Snake" Roberts, who was at the time presented as a born-again Christian character. Austin's merciless and clinical beatdown of a sympathetic legend in the match itself was textbook heel behavior, and his victory interview was even more so:

Dok Hendrix: The fourth prestigious King Of The Ring, Stone Cold Steve Austin, an incredible victory!

Steve Austin: The first thing I want to be done, is to get that piece of crap out of my ring. Don't just get him out of the ring, get him out of the WWF because I've proved son, without a shadow of a doubt, you ain't got what it takes anymore! You sit there and you thump your Bible, and you say your prayers, and it didn't get you anywhere. Talk about your psalms, talk about John 3:16 . . . Austin 3:16 says I just whipped your ass!

Hendrix: Come on, that's not necessary.

Austin: All he's gotta do is go buy him a cheap bottle of Thunderbird and try to dig back some of that courage he had in his prime. As the King Of The Ring, I'm serving notice to every one of the WWF superstars. I don't give a damn what they are, they're all on the list, and that's Stone Cold's list, and I'm fixing to start running through all of 'em. And as far as this championship match is considered son, I don't give a damn if it's Davey Boy Smith or Shawn Michaels, Steve Austin's time is come, and when I get that shot you're looking at the next WWF Champion. And that's the bottom line, because Stone Cold said so.

Hendrix: Obviously anything but humble, the fourth prestigious King Of The Ring, Stone Cold Steve Austin! (WWF King of the Ring 1996, *WWE Network*)

Trashing a beloved legend, and mocking his religious beliefs?! Forming a catchphrase that – as Jeff Jarrett pointed out on an episode of Monday Night Raw – is borderline blasphemy?! Surely these are the actions of a dastardly heel to be booed out the building in the normally pious United States! Not so. Whilst Austin did continue to be booed as a heel, the audience started responding more positively to his character, and the "Austin 3:16 says I just whipped your ass" catchphrase became more and more popular. When the "Austin 3:16" T-shirt was released, it became one of the biggest-selling pieces of wrestling merchandise ever, and became ubiquitous on WWF television, and beyond.

Austin's popularity grew, and he started getting cheers even when pitted against a legend and long-time babyface Bret "Hitman" Hart, who was returning to action after an extended absence. Surely battling with the Hitman would make the boos for Austin louder than the cheers? Not quite. Even though Austin was booed in their first match at Survivor Series in November 1996, there were still notable cheers and Austin 3:16 signs in the crowd. Even after he lost to Bret, his popularity didn't suffer. Austin and Bret's feud continued into early 1997, with Austin cheating Bret out of a win in the 1997 Royal Rumble. Austin then went on to cost Bret his WWF title against Sycho Sid, setting up a brutal submission match between the two at WrestleMania 13 in the spring of 1997.

At this point, WWF management had noticed that Austin's popularity was waxing, and Bret's was waning. No matter how dastardly Austin behaved, it didn't slow down the growing cheers from the crowd. At WrestleMania 13, the WWF decided to execute a rare "double turn", where Bret would turn heel, and Austin would turn babyface, in the same match. This was delivered perfectly in a match that is widely considered to be one of the best of all time. After an intense bout, which saw Austin "busted open" and bleeding profusely, Bret had Austin tied up in his signature sharpshooter submission move. Austin tried desperately to break the hold, but couldn't. However, in a classic babyface move, he refused to submit. Eventually Austin passed out, and the match was awarded to Hart, but not because of a submission. Hart then started further beating down the unconscious Austin, drawing boos, before backing down from a confrontation with the guest referee, former UFC champion Ken Shamrock, drawing further boos for cowardice. Austin, due to his epic display of fortitude, was cheered as he walked out the ring on his own steam.

This allowed the WWF to present Austin as a babyface, and built him up as one in superb fashion. In a key move, they didn't remove many of the heelish aspects of his character that made him popular. Austin continued to attack people at random, including announcers; continued to curse on TV; and continued to viciously and remorselessly pursue his opponents. Austin fast became the most popular babyface in the entire company, with crowd reactions to the glass

Table 4. Austin in 1999.

Sphere of Action or Feeling	Excess	Mean	Deficiency
Fear and Confidence	**Rashness**	Courage	Cowardice
Pleasure and Pain	Licentiousness/ Self-indulgence	Temperance	**Insensibility**
Getting and Spending (minor)	Prodigality	**Liberality**	Illiberality/Meanness
Getting and Spending (major)	**Vulgarity/ Tastelessness**	Magnificence	Pettiness/Stinginess
Honor and Dishonor (major)	Vanity	**Magnanimity**	Pusillanimity
Honor and Dishonor (minor)	Ambition/Empty vanity	**Proper ambition/ Pride**	Unambitiousness/ Undue humility
Anger	**Irascibility**	Patience/Good temper	Lack of spirit/ Unirascibility
Self-expression	**Boastfulness**	Truthfulness	Understatement/Mock modesty
Conversation	Buffoonery	**Wittiness**	Boorishness
Social Conduct	Obsequiousness	Friendliness	**Cantankerousness**
Shame	Shyness	Modesty	**Shamelessness**
Indignation	Envy	Righteous indignation	**Malicious enjoyment/ Spitefulness**

breaking at the start of his entrance music being deafening. Austin would go on to be possibly the biggest star in wrestling history.

If we use the classic criteria of virtue and vice, Austin would be a clear heel. Indeed, if we look at the list of virtues and vices in Table 4, we can see that Austin exhibited more vices than virtues.

What Austin's status as a babyface showed was that vices were no longer just for heels, and the classic alignment of babyface with virtue and heel with vice had been disrupted.

What did this character tap into that made it so popular? First of all, it is worth noting that there was a general shift in the audience's responses of which Austin was a part. The traditional "white meat" babyfaces who were wholesome, plucky underdogs that told the audience to "say their prayers, eat their vitamins, and drink their milk" were no longer being accepted by the crowd (indeed, Kurt Angle would use these phrases to great effect as a heel in the early 2000s). It could be because these characters were originally aimed at children, who, since watching Hulk Hogan in the late 1980s and early 1990s, were now young adults who wanted something a little more edgy. If the WWF's audience had grown up, the WWF realized it had to grow up with them, and create characters that were more resonant with the rebellion of the teenage/early twenties years of American males. This time of life is often one of rejection of one's parents and one's childhood. One is keen to assert that one is "not a kid anymore", and will tear down posters of childhood heroes and replace them with something new, and sometimes completely the opposite. If you loved Hulk Hogan's wholesome message as a kid, you might be looking for something totally the opposite when a teenager or a young adult.

To keep the audience it had cultivated as kids in the late 1980s and early 1990s, the WWF realized it needed to change its product. It was under pressure from WCW's nWo storyline, complete with a heel "Hollywood" Hogan, and the smaller ECW promotion, based in Philadelphia, which developed a cult following of its violent and edgy low-budget shows. This change in "attitude" was famously heralded by the following speech by WWF owner Vince McMahon on Monday Night Raw on December 15, 1997:

> We in the WWF think that you, the audience, are quite frankly, tired of having your intelligence insulted. We also think that you're tired of the same old simplistic theory of "good guys vs bad guys". Surely the era of the super-hero urging you to "say your prayers and take your vitamins" is definitely, passé. Therefore, we've embarked on a far more innovative and contemporary creative campaign, that is far more invigorating and extemporaneous than ever before. However, due to the live nature of Raw and the War Zone, we encourage some degree of parental discretion, as relates to the younger audience allowed to stay up late. (WWF Monday Night Raw, December 15, 1997, *WWE Network*)

McMahon's explicit acknowledgment of the change in direction of the WWF was a risky move as, like his interview after the Montreal Screwjob, it broke kayfabe, but the "Attitude Era" it precipitated was one of the most successful periods in the company's history.

A surefire way to get heat as a heel in this new world was to be the thing that this audience resented the most: the authority figure. Whether it's the parents or teacher of a teenager, or the boss of a young adult, authority figures represented all that was to be fought against: the person who tried to impose their outdated values on you, or took delight in their ability to make you do what you didn't want to do. Many people had this fantasy of rebellion against such figures, and the WWF exploited that with great success. Thus, the evil boss "Mr McMahon" character was born, and proved the perfect foil to Austin.

The attitude of Austin as an insubordinate rebel is encapsulated in this exchange with Vince McMahon after Austin had won the WWF Championship. McMahon is telling Austin that, now that he's champion, he needs to step in line with the corporate way of doing things:

Steve Austin: . . . What I'm telling you – and you can look right in my bloodshot eyes – I ain't gonna do things your way. I will continue to raise as much hell and do things, and create as much chaos and give you more grey hairs every single day of your life. Nobody . . . nobody, especially Vince McMahon, tells Stone Cold Steve Austin what to do, and that's the bottom line!

Vince McMahon: Well, we can either do this the easy way or we can do this the hard way, Mr. Austin. And that's gonna be your decision.

Austin: Well, that . . . that sounds like an important decision. The easy way or the hard way. If I'm gonna be able to be forced to make a decision here tonight, I'd like your definition of what the easy way and what the hard way is. What is your definition of that?

McMahon: It's real simple. The easy way is to learn to be flexible, to learn to adapt, Mr. Austin, and – if you'd bear with me for just a moment, please – Mr. Austin, adaptation is a key of life as well as in business. That's the easy way and, quite frankly, the hard way – You're gonna wind up doing it my way anyhow, you'd be forced into doing it my way, so that's the hard way, and we don't even need to discuss that.

Austin: Like I said: That's an extremely important decision in

my book for yours and my relationship. Can I have maybe ten
seconds to think about this decision?

McMahon: By all means.

[Austin kicks Vince in the gut, then hits him with a Stone Cold
Stunner.]

Austin: What you've just seen – What you've seen is how to do
things the hard way. If you want Stone Cold to continue doing
things the hard way, gimme a hell yeah! [crowd shouts "Hell
yeah!"] Oh hell yeah! (WWF Raw is War, March 30, 1998, *WWE
Network*)

What McMahon is asking Austin to do here is the conventional thing:
when you're the champion, there is a set of rules you have to follow.
You're a corporate entity now, and you have to act in a corporate way.
Austin must leave his hell-raising days behind him, and embrace the
new role he has now that he's champion. This is the "easy way" that
he describes.

Here we see Austin living out the rebellious fantasy. First of all,
telling the boss that he won't do what he's told, listening to the boss's
attempts to convince him otherwise, and then responding with a
more emphatic rejection; a physical attack – a Stone Cold Stunner.
Of course, usually this would lead to the employee being fired, and
McMahon would "fire" Austin in storylines many times during this
period, but Austin would always find a way to outsmart the boss and
re-take his position.

Evil "authority" figures have continued to be used in pro wrestling,
particularly WWE, even encapsulated in the group "The Authority" of
Stephanie McMahon and Triple H. Raging against authority figures,
usually members of the McMahon family, not only helped make the
career of Steve Austin, but also, almost 20 years later in the 2010s,

helped make such stars as CM Punk, Daniel Bryan, Roman Reigns, Becky Lynch, Kofi Kingston, Seth Rollins, and Kevin Owens. Indeed, Becky Lynch's rise to stardom in 2018 bore a number of similarities with the Austin–McMahon storylines, with Lynch refusing to be intimidated by Stephanie McMahon and Triple H, and even physically attacking them, much as Austin had done with Vince McMahon. All of these characters, who became megastars, were flawed: none were the classic Hogan-esque babyfaces of old, but this was not a barrier to their success. On the contrary, their flaws made them *even more* popular than babyface characters who were not given vices and layers of complexity.

5. Reflecting on the Disruption

The classic battle between good and evil, of perfect virtue versus inherent vice, thus transformed into a more complex arena of flawed heroes fighting new kinds of enemies. When presented with a choice between a wholly virtuous character, and a character that exhibited a number of vices, audiences started to choose the characters with vices. Indeed, many of the most popular babyface characters would exhibit a mix of virtues and vices, including vices classically associated with heels. Characters such as The Rock and Chris Jericho became popular partly because of their extravagance, a feature marking heels in the days of Ric Flair in the 1980s. Making fun of people, particularly those weaker than oneself, was also not a bar to popularity, a practice The Rock frequently engaged in with interviewers backstage, such as naming Kevin Kelly "Hermy", the hermaphrodite. Becky Lynch's popularity in 2018 came partly from her relentless and vicious pursuit of Charlotte Flair, along with her cockiness on the mic, calling Ronda Rousey "Ronnie".

However, there are some features that are constant amongst baby-faces, and what this shows is not that virtue does not matter, but rather that there are some core virtues that cannot fail to be exhibited for a character to serve as a babyface. Cowardice, in particular, seems to be something that still marks out a heel, as none of the babyface characters in this new world are cowards. Pride is a key factor for babyfaces, and, indeed, one of the key strikes heel characters make against these babyfaces are pride-based: attempting to take away something key to their personal pride, whether it be a championship or some other personal item. Wittiness is also important, as part of what makes the crowd love a character is that they make them laugh, or show up their opponents verbally: a character who is not able to hold their own on the mic is less likely to be popular.

So, if you can display courage (or rashness), pride, and wittiness, many vices can be forgiven. No longer do characters have to be whole-some, family-friendly, perfectly virtuous individuals; they can exhibit many vices, so long as they have a particular core of virtues that pri-marily guide their characters.

Why is this? Is it because the Aristotelian ideal is not what people want? Does it show a startling decline in moral values? Does it show that nobody cares about being good any more? Or, is it because char-acters with vices are more realistic, more relatable? Indeed, as we saw above, one complaint commonly made about wrestling prior to this shift was that it was *too* cartoonish, *too* unbelievable. People craved more reality in their shows, and characters of Aristotelian perfection are just too unrealistic to be interesting.

When one reads Aristotle's description of the virtuous person, and the lifetime of effort required to achieve this, it's hard to resist the thought that this person is just a bit *too* much of a goody-two-shoes. Obviously, we should all work to better ourselves, but to do so with continual effort, and an attempt to remove *all* vices? This does sound quite distant from the reality of the lives we live. This could be the very same thought that drives the negative reactions to John Cena, along with the change in fan reaction to Hulk Hogan in the mid-1990s that led to his heel turn. For Aristotle, this wasn't necessarily a problem, as for him, only those with the necessary time and training (i.e. philosophers) were really able to achieve this goal, so it's hardly surprising that it seems distant and unrelatable to most people.

This points us to an interesting change in the relationship between philosophy and pro wrestling. Philosophy is to a large extent about ideals: the ideally good person; the ideally good circumstances for knowledge. For a while, pro wrestling was about ideals too: ideals of physique, of good and bad characters. But audiences tired of these ideals; they wanted something more real, more gritty, more relatable.

The thought thus is that this shift away from the classic view of morality in wrestling, and its Aristotelian ideals, is not necessarily a sign of moral abandonment or decay. Instead, it signifies a move toward providing moral exemplars that the audience can relate to, and can more realistically aspire to be like. We are not looking for flawless saints; instead, what we want are people like us, who are just that little bit better, with the thought that with some small and manageable changes in our lives, we can become better people.

5

Justice: Prejudice vs Progress

WrestleMania 35 began with a rather intense display of patriotism. As "America the Beautiful" rang out, 80,000 people were on their feet, and four military helicopters hovered above the stadium. The man to my left, who had had his hand on his heart throughout, and looked bemused by the fact that me and my friend Chris did not, turned to me with a big grin and shouted "bad ass", twice, right in my ear. When the show started, the host – Alexa Bliss – promised a "WrestleMania moment", clicked her fingers, and Hulk Hogan's music hit. Hogan had been on a hiatus from WWE for a few years prior when a tape emerged of Terry Bollea, the man behind Hulk Hogan, using appalling racist language, but WWE were gradually bringing the character back into view. This had been a controversial move, for which WWE had been heavily criticized, including by its own performers of color, particularly as Bollea had not offered a satisfactory apology for what he said.

Despite knowing all this, I followed those around me in getting to my feet – after all, it's *Hulk Hogan*, at *WrestleMania*! As I looked around, though, I saw two young black men to my friend's right, who were sat down looking at the floor. I suddenly felt a deep sense of shame, and sat down. I thought to myself: "How could I have forgotten everything for a cheap pop?".

Later that night, Kofi Kingston won the WWE Championship from Daniel Bryan in a wonderful match, and gave us a very rare occurrence:

a black WWE champion. The story leading up to the match had been one filled with racial undertones, including the suggestion that Kofi was only a "B+ player", with a natural ceiling that would prevent him from getting to the top. Kingston even said to Vince McMahon in a SmackDown TV segment that "I've never complained about the fact that you have never allowed someone like me to compete or contend for the WWE title." Obstacle after obstacle was placed in his way by the nefarious "Mr McMahon", before Kofi was finally able to earn his opportunity. At least, in this case, the story ended with Kofi winning, unlike a previous storyline WWE had run with Triple H and Booker T at WrestleMania 19. That build-up featured more explicitly racist comments from Triple H, using comments like "nappy hair", saying that "I think you're a bit confused about your role in life . . . somebody like you doesn't get to be a world champion", and asking Booker T to "dance for me". This alone was inexcusable, but what many took further issue with was that Triple H ended up beating Booker after all this, thus effectively vindicating the racist narrative he had been spinning beforehand.

Since WrestleMania 35, Bollea has apparently offered more sincere apologies to some WWE performers for what he said, but the lack of a public apology is notable and Hogan has been on WWE TV many times. There is no doubt that pro wrestling has a problematic history when it comes to race, and these issues need to be confronted properly. As we saw earlier in the discussion of morality, justice is a key concept in pro wrestling storylines: the heels must get their comeuppance and the babyfaces must prevail. What we will focus on here is the issue of *social justice*, and some examples of the ways the issues of race and sexuality have been presented in pro wrestling. If you're unfamiliar with the uglier side of pro wrestling's history, I should warn you that some of the events discussed here are pretty shocking.

1. Race and Jingoism in Pro Wrestling

Wrestling in most countries is a fairly insular phenomenon. In America, the WWF in the 1980s and 1990s typically pitted a wholesome American character against an evil foreign enemy, whether they be Russian, German, Iranian, Japanese, or Iraqi. There was a clear distinction between good guys and bad guys on nationalistic grounds: if an American was fighting a foreigner, the American would be cheered, and the foreigner booed. Whilst American wrestling companies are frequently lampooned for this, it is a practice common in other countries too. In Japan, for example, foreign wrestlers, called *gaijin*, were typically heels taking on homegrown Japanese heroes. The *gaijin's* refusal to speak Japanese, or engage in the cultural traditions of Japanese wrestling were just as despicable to the fans as waving the Iraqi flag was on WWF TV. In Mexico, *gringo* performers were often portrayed as heels (or *rudos*), and the Japanese star Tetsuya Naito developed his signature pose, in which he holds one eye open between finger and thumb, in response to Mexican fans shouting "open your eyes".

This jingoistic aspect of some wrestling time periods and companies is problematic in itself, but, when it becomes combined with issues of race, it is especially so. There are numerous examples of non-white characters being portrayed as violent savages, such as the disturbing and offensive character Kamala, the "Ugandan Giant" of the WWF and WCW in the late 1980s/early 1990s, who was billed as coming from darkest Africa, and appeared in a loincloth, tribal facepaint, with a "handler" Kim Chee: a white man in an explorer's outfit. The same era saw the Samoan team The Headshrinkers, and the witch doctor Papa Shango. Characters from Mexico and Japan were frequently the butt of racist jokes on commentary.

Rarely are issues of race directly addressed in pro wrestling. Even the late 1990s WWF stable, the Nation of Domination, populated by black stars making the black power salute, steered more toward implicit associations with the Nation of Islam, rather than explicitly addressing racial issues on air. It shouldn't be ignored, too, that they were presented as bad guys. One time when racial issues were directly discussed, which ended in great controversy, was the Muhammad Hassan character featured in WWE in 2004–5. Hassan was portrayed as an Arab-American, who was distressed by the discrimination and prejudice faced by Arab-Americans in the wake of 9/11. Here is the text of an initial vignette introducing the character:

Hello. My name is Muhammad Hassan. I am an Arab-American. I grew up right here in America. But since 9/11, you people tend to generalize, or stereotype people like me. But I implore you, please, don't confuse me with acts of terrorism here in America and around the world. I am asking you people to please just give me the opportunity to represent you, and the WWE. Thank you. Praise Allah. Now please be respectful as my manager, Khosrow Daivari, translates for our Arab brothers. (*WWE Monday Night RAW, November 1, 2004, WWE Network*)

Hassan, along with his manager Daivari, cut increasingly angry promos discussing how racial discrimination had forced Arab-Americans to close their businesses, and feel threatened when traveling, or walking down the street, explaining that he would be forced to turn to violence if he wasn't treated properly. His promo, broadcast on WWE.com just after the July 7, 2005 attacks in London, after which the character was removed from TV, was very interesting, both because of what he said and the crowd's reactions:

I stand here tonight, probably the last true patriot in America. I stand here tonight perhaps even a martyr against tyranny and injustice. Because the fact is, I am an *American* professional wrestler. But, because of my heritage, because of my background, because of who my ancestors were, I am (we're) labeled a terrorist . . .

The point is . . . because of the fear that the media puts in you people, I have been denied my God-given right to pursue the profession of my choice; to pursue the American dream. I have been denied my basic rights as an American citizen. [The crowd boos.]

You know, as I look around this crowd, and I look at all these faces looking back at me in disgust, I think a lot of you people have forgotten what this country was founded on. I think, all of you people have forgotten that your ancestors fought for their freedom, they gave their lives for their freedom. Whether they be black, Irish-American, Italian American, Jewish American, Asian American, they gave their lives for their freedoms. What's next people, what's next? Because any time anything goes wrong in this country, it's the Arabs. When a plane crashes, it's the Arabs. When a bomb goes off, it's the Arabs. The blackout two summers ago, it was the Arabs. Hurricane Dennis, must be the Arabs. [The crowd starts chanting "USA, USA!".]

You people, say what you want, because I have a right to be in here, I have a right to say what I want. And what I want to say, my name is Muhammad Hassan, I am an Arab-American, and I am very proud of my heritage (crowd boos). But as an American, my first amendment rights have been trampled, and I stand here before all of you ashamed of my country. [The crowd boos.]

From the character's point of view, Hassan was a person fighting against racial injustice, and there is no doubt that the message Hassan was conveying was an important one: America is a country with deep racial divides, and significant racial injustice. These injustices are often invisible to the white majority, who do not experience the sorts of things that make life difficult for those with darker skin tones. Making those experiences vivid and urgent is a key part of addressing these injustices, in that many people need to be made aware of them before they can be addressed.

However, this reasonable and important message about racial injustice was being presented by people the audience was conditioned to boo. Hassan and Daivari were set up as devious heels, attacking announcers Jim Ross and Jerry Lawler, interrupting Mick Foley's promo about *Tribute to the Troops,* and kicking Stacy Kiebler out the ring. All of these actions were designed to make the audience boo them: attacking beloved "All-American" announcers, disrespecting the troops, and denying the audience their glimpse of a scantily clad woman. Thus, the crowd was conditioned to boo them by their actions, in addition to their "Arab" appearance, removing any doubt that these were bad guys.

Hassan was thus presenting the prejudices of the audience to them, being booed for it, *and this was the intended reaction.* The way WWE presented the issues, the oppressors – the prejudiced audience – were the *good guys,* reveling in their disapproval for the victimized oppressed, the Arab-Americans. Far from prompting people to think critically about their views and engage seriously with issues of racial injustice, WWE was instead highlighting these issues and then *reinforcing* the audience's racist beliefs. *America* is just *White America,* and anyone of color who complains should "leave it", regardless of their citizenship status. This is worse than not raising the issues at all.

It is important to note that (White) America is not particularly comfortable with self-critique. Even when there are significant social problems to be addressed, it is rare to see these ideas expressed as problems with America *as a country*. This makes audiences (and voters) turn against anyone, including white men, who explicitly question the greatness of America (as seen when Governor of New York, Andrew Cuomo, said that America was "never that great" in August 2018). When it is done by someone who is not viewed as part of mainstream America, such as a person of color, this typically prompts a hysterically negative reaction from a certain portion of white Americans (think, for example, of the reaction to Colin Kaepernick's anthem protests in 2016). In wrestling history, the phrase "America: love it or leave it" has been used frequently, and to very positive crowd reactions, since Shawn Michaels uttered it to Bret Hart in 1997, and it was wheeled out again in the Hassan storyline. It is important to remember, though, that the essence of this phrase is *"White* America: Love it or Leave It", and this should make you uneasy no matter how patriotic you are.

It is often said in wrestling that the best heels are those who "tell the truth". A good heel should be justified – by his or her lights – in their actions, and this is all the more powerful if what they say is true. Heels are supposed to make their opponents, and the audience who cheers their opponents – uncomfortable, and tell them some difficult truths about themselves. There is a big difference, though, between the kinds of truths heels had told before – that their opponent's best days were behind them, or that their opponent wasn't a real hero, that they didn't deserve the title, or that no-one really liked them – and the sorts of truths Hassan was telling. First of all, the traditional heel truths are designed to give the babyface something to overcome: perhaps Kenny Omega is right that Hiroshi Tanahashi's best days are behind him, but that gives Tanahashi something to overcome if he is to beat Omega. Perhaps Sasha Banks was right that Bayley had fallen behind, but that makes Bayley's ability to succeed even more impressive. Perhaps Austin was right that Whipwreck was not a worthy champion, but that makes Mikey's victory even more powerful. The truths aren't irrelevant, but nor are they decisive: they provide obstacles for the babyfaces to overcome, thereby making their victories more significant.

The sorts of truths that Hassan was telling, though, are precisely the sorts of things that *should not* be overcome in that sense. They should not be things that their babyface opponents overcome in order to make their victories sweeter. It is not as though Hulk Hogan and Shawn Michaels *overcame* truths about racial injustice for Arab-Americans to beat Hassan and Daivari. On the contrary: when Hassan and Daivari were beaten up by their white babyface opponents, this was a way of making the truths they told *irrelevant*. The message was: "don't worry if what Hassan says makes you uncomfortable, you're white Americans damnit, and you're right in your beliefs, and here comes Hulk Hogan to prove it! Get ready now. . . . USA! USA! USA!".

The purpose of the beatdown of the heels here was not to show that uncomfortable truths can be overcome, but rather to *silence* the telling of those truths, and show that they were not relevant in the first place. In fact, we might doubt whether WWE was even *presenting these things as truths* given the way what Hassan said was intended to be taken. For one thing, the announcers showed little if any sympathy for Hassan's claims, as they occasionally do with things other heels say. Nor did their opponents acknowledge the veracity of their claims, as babyfaces did in other cases. Veteran babyface wrestlers, for example, would often acknowledge the heel young upstart's claim – "maybe I am past my best, but I can still beat you!" – but this didn't happen with Hassan. Instead he was constantly met with jingoistic "love it or leave it" lines. The closest was when John Cena denied that he didn't like him because he was Arab-American, but rather because he was "Asshole-American". Obviously, the crowd loved this too, but it did not engage with Hassan's primary message about the plight of *all* Arab-Americans, not just himself.

Finally, there is a troubling trope in wrestling history of stereotypical characters being portrayed by people who did not share the character's ethnic origin, such as Chief Jay Strongbow, a Native American character portrayed by an Italian American; Akeem the African Dream, played by a Caucasian; and Yokozuna, a Japanese character portrayed by a Samoan American. If the Hassan storyline was intended to be a serious attempt to portray racial injustice from an Arab-American perspective, the performer who played Hassan should not be a white person pretending to be of Arab-American origin, and dressing in stereotypical Arab costume. Unfortunately, this seems to be what happened, with the performer stating in an interview with WrestlingInc.com in 2016 that he is "100% Italian".

Hassan's storyline occurred in the mid-2000s, which is over 10 years ago now. Have things improved? In some respects, pro wrestling seems better placed than it was then. In New Japan, for example, it is not the case that overseas performers are necessarily heels, and some – such as Kenny Omega and Will Ospreay – became fan favorites. In WWE, the issues are complex. Whilst performers of color undoubtedly take on more prominent roles, there is still a temptation to revert to the stereotypes of old. Jinder Mahal's run as WWE Champion in 2017, for example, very explicitly branded him, and his minions, the Singh brothers, as Indian (even though Mahal is from Canada, of Indian descent), and much of his promos involved him running down the American audience before a white American performer would answer the call of the crowd to challenge him. Kofi Kingston's WWE

Championship win in 2019 was an important moment, but one long overdue, and it remains to be seen whether it will lead to sustained periods at the top for black performers. We will discuss approaches to race in contemporary pro wrestling more below, but for now I want to turn to discuss issues of sexuality.

2. LGBTQ Issues in Pro Wrestling

Much like race, LGBTQ issues have not been treated well in the history of pro wrestling. In this section we'll focus on a couple of significant cases in WWE that took place in the same week in 2002.

The Billy and Chuck storyline featured in the WWF and WWE from 2001 to 2002, and involved the characters Billy Gunn and Chuck Palumbo. In 2001, after a period of success as part of D-Generation X as "Bad Ass" Billy Gunn, Gunn's career was stalling a little, and he was paired with Chuck Palumbo, a recent acquisition from the now-defunct WCW. As a tag team, they were presented as "Billy and Chuck", and were soon given a number of homoerotic vignettes to present their characters. They were often seen in questionable training poses, and were given a "personal stylist", named Rico, as a manager. Billy and Chuck, in line with other characters with homosexual overtones, were presented as heels, with the fans' boos increasing as they hammed up the homoeroticism in the ring.

A key development in the story was Chuck's proposal to Billy to be his "tag team partner for life". Palumbo got down on one knee after a match, and proposed to Gunn, offering him a ring. Gunn accepted, despite the notable chants of "no, no, no!" from the crowd. A gay relationship was being explicitly presented as something to be rejected and booed by the crowd, who were more than happy to oblige.

The culmination of the storyline was the "wedding" on the September 12, 2002 episode of WWE SmackDown. In-ring wedding ceremonies were not unusual on WWE TV, but this would be the first gay wedding ceremony featured. The ring was decorated as a wedding chapel, and Billy and Chuck were dressed in suits. Once again, the crowd heavily booed the idea of Billy and Chuck being married, and cheered interruptions to the ceremony.

One interrupter was "The Godfather", a pimp character, who came to the ring complete with his "Ho train" of prostitutes. Troubling as well was the wild popularity of this character, despite the ugly racial stereotype it perpetrated, and the casual misogyny it involved. Concerningly, this character still pops up on WWE TV in nostalgia shows, most recently in the "Raw Reunion" show in July 2019.

The Godfather asked Billy and Chuck, "what happened?", drawing cheers from the audience at the mention of their heterosexual past. The Godfather urged them to go back to this, offering them the services of his ladies. Billy and Chuck seemed tempted, and the crowd were encouraging them to do so, but their stylist Rico sent the Godfather away. As the ceremony progressed, Billy and Chuck looked increasingly uncomfortable, but proceedings were pushed along by Rico. At the part where they were to exchange vows, a reluctant Gunn and Palumbo did so. However, the crowd cheered as Palumbo said to Rico that this was just supposed to be a publicity stunt, and he and Gunn categorically said that they were not gay, and looked disgusted by the prospect. After this, it was revealed that the minister conducting the ceremony was actually the dastardly WWE Raw General Manager Eric Bischoff in disguise, and he called in his minions, the team 3 Minute Warning, to lay waste to the entire group of people in the ring, including Billy and Chuck.

This was an alarming segment. The fact that Billy and Chuck's rejection of being gay was presented as a babyface move to be cheered, and being gay was presented as something bad, and to be avoided, was terrible. (It was also not the first time this had happened in the company, as Goldust's face turn in 1996 came when his resounding "no!" to Jerry Lawler's question of whether he was "a queer" brought cheers from the audience.) Also disturbing was the Godfather's intervention to try to steer Billy and Chuck back to the "straight and narrow", with the additional implication that being gay or straight is a choice that a person has control over. Finally, as we will return to below, the fact that the segment ended in violence toward these characters, was incredibly disturbing. This was an outright rejection of the idea that being gay is acceptable, done in a very offensive and derogatory way.

Here is what wrestler Mike Parrow had to say about how disturbing this was to him at the time as a young gay person, in Graham Isador's July 2019 article on vice.com:

> It was very difficult. I often talk about how the Chuck and Billy storyline [where two straight wrestlers pretended to be gay in order to enrage the crowd] affected me greatly, more than I even knew. Because it was the first time as a closeted teenager I saw characters similar to me . . . and when it ended the way it did it made me feel that wrestling did not respect LGBTQ wrestlers.

It's unclear what WWE's initial plans were for this storyline. WWE producer Bruce Prichard, in Episode 48 of *Something to Wrestle with Bruce Prichard*, for example, suggested that the original plan was for Billy and Chuck to get married, but that Vince McMahon got cold feet and changed the ending. Indeed, this original plan was believed by the Gay and Lesbian Alliance Against Defamation (GLAAD) to be the case, and GLAAD was very critical of WWE when the show was broadcast. Scott Seomin of GLAAD said in 2002:

> The WWE lied to us two months ago when they promised that Billy & Chuck would come out and wed on the air. In fact, I was told (lied to) the day after the show was taped in Minneapolis that the wedding took place and all was well.

History might have looked a little differently at this storyline if the wedding had gone through, but the fact remains that the characters – all along – were presented as heels for the crowd to boo and jeer, and, moreover, that they were to be jeered precisely because of their presumed homosexual identities.

Moreover, whatever the original plans, this segment took place *in the same week* as a segment on WWE Monday Night Raw promising "Hot Lesbian Action" ("HLA"). On the September 9, 2002 episode of Raw, Raw General Manager Eric Bischoff introduced two characters, simply called "The Lesbians", who were played by local wrestlers. They came to the ring, and, at the sleazy encouragement of Bischoff, stripped each other down to their underwear, and started to kiss. Before long, they were brutally attacked by Bischoff's aforementioned goons 3 Minute Warning, who beat the women up, and left them lying unconscious in the ring.

This was another highly disturbing segment. The women's identity as "the Lesbians" was solely based on their role of titillating the male audience looking on. Their affection for each other was simply a vehicle for male gratification, just as Billy and Chuck's affection for each other was a vehicle for male disgust. These were also two segments in the same week where there was a significant physical assault on characters presented as gay. Considering the appalling violence inflicted on gay people precisely because they are gay, the idea of this being presented as entertainment is chilling. As we noted in the discussion of intergender wrestling above, there are some things that it's not acceptable to do to generate heel heat. There we talked about racism, domestic violence, and sexual assault, and here we can add to that list homophobic character presentation and the beating up of apparently gay characters when their sexuality is at issue.

Vince McMahon, on the September 14, 2002 episode of *WWE Confidential* addressing the controversy with these segments, did acknowledge that what he called the "physicality" of the "HLA" segment (i.e. the assault of two gay women by two burly men) may have gone too far, though he did try to defend WWE from charges of what he called "gay-bashing" on the grounds that the same men had also beaten up elderly women and midgets. If this seems glaringly insufficient, his defense of the Billy and Chuck segment was just as baffling. He seemed to think that the controversy was about WWE showing a gay wedding, and defends the WWE's right to show a gay wedding, without at all addressing the fact that the wedding *did not* take place, and that the characters ended up denying that they were gay in the first place.

3. Reflecting Culture vs Changing It

Another part of WWE's defense at the time was that, in Vince McMahon's words on the aforementioned 2002 episode of *WWE Confidential*, "I think our television program has to reflect what's going on in society." The apparent defense here is that if the show features homophobic material, that's down to society not WWE, who are just presenting what they see. Indeed, in Lia Miller's *New York*

Times article of July 18, 2005, WWE's response to criticism of the Hassan storyline reinforcing stereotypes of Arab-Americans was "It is these stereotypical images that many people hold that we hope to debunk as part of the Hassan's story."

This idea of reflecting society is not an uncommon view of what pro wrestling involves. As legendary wrestler and best-selling author Mick Foley puts it (in a different context), "wrestling is, and always has been, a mirror of the times we live in" (Foley 2001: 41). However, we will see that this is not a satisfactory justification for these segments in these contexts, and thinking about why it's not will help us get a handle on what the responsibilities of pro wrestling companies are.

The first issue concerns the general idea that companies can satisfy themselves with just reflecting the social mores of the day. Mirroring the times can help businesses by making their product relatable to the audience, and to advertisers. However, is this really an excuse when the times we live in contain problematic elements that should be critiqued? Pro wrestling, as an art form, has an opportunity not just to engage in cultural reflection, but also in cultural critique. There is power here: as Oscar Wilde famously put it, "Life imitates Art far more than Art imitates Life". Pro wrestling does not need to just pander to fans' views; it can also ask fans to reflect on their views, and look to change them.

Mirroring reality *can* effect social change by laying bare the ugliness of a culture for all to see, but this requires careful presentation to show that the things presented *are* problems. In particular, the mirroring needs to challenge the viewer to re-examine the prejudices they have, as opposed to reinforcing problematic pre-existing views. This is something it's fairly easy to see in pro wrestling, as characters are – more often than not – presented to the audience in a way that suggests whether they should cheer them or boo them. Certainly, the examples of Billy and Chuck and Muhammad Hassan fall into the category of reinforcing problematic pre-existing views, in that the ways the characters were presented to the audience (as characters to be booed, and the reasons why they were to be booed) were designed to align with pre-existing homophobic and racist views. If the characters had been presented in a more sympathetic light so that the audience was encouraged to at least see their point of view and feel something other than animosity towards them, then it would have been a different story.

So, claiming to just be "mirroring the times" is a very weak defense: even if we suppose that the storylines were mirroring a racist and homophobic society, this doesn't excuse the pandering to racism and homophobia that they involved. It may explain why WWE thought it was OK to show these characters and storylines, but it doesn't justify them in a way that constitutes a defense.

Moreover, properly mirroring the times requires seriously presenting more than one point of view, and this didn't happen in these cases. Failing to present the points of view of gay people (as in the Billy and Chuck storyline), or seriously acknowledge the plight of people of color (as in the Hassan storyline), doesn't mirror the whole of reality, it just reflects one part of it – in these cases, the dominant white racist and homophobic part. The idea that WWE was just mirroring society is simply false.

The second issue here is that, even if we buy into the dubious "mirroring the times" idea, it doesn't explain the minimal LGBTQ representation in WWE since 2002. In 2019 there is a notable lack of LGBTQ characters and storylines on WWE TV, despite Stephanie McMahon's 2016 promise that there would be. Even when there have been openly gay wrestlers, such as Darren Young and Sonya Deville, there has been little attempt to acknowledge this, or use it in storylines.

Whilst Sonya Deville does wear rainbow gear, and talks about her sexuality on behind-the-scenes shows, it is not openly acknowledged in the main TV shows. We get Finn Balor's "Balor Club is for Everyone" rainbow attire and merchandising, but this is not connected to anything explicitly acknowledged about Balor's character, or an LGBTQ storyline (Balor did have representatives of the New Orleans LGBTQ community present during his entrance at WrestleMania 34, but there was no tie to his character or storylines). Likewise for the annual special edition Pride-based T-shirts WWE offers: they appear on shows where there is little to no acknowledged LGBTQ representation or storylines.

Why is this so, and does this reflect WWE's deeper ambivalence, or even hostility, to LGBTQ issues? This question is particularly acute given the McMahons' conservative political leanings, and WWE's proximity to Donald Trump, and the Trump administration, which has proved hostile to the LGBTQ community. Trump is in the WWE Hall of Fame after decades of business dealings with the company, and Linda McMahon, former CEO of WWE and wife of Vince McMahon, served as a member of Trump's cabinet, as the small business administrator, before chairing a Political Action Committee (PAC) for his re-election. WWE also has a significant business relationship with Saudi Arabia, where homosexuality is a crime. Thus, these concerns persist even in spite of WWE's reconciliation with GLAAD and annual issuing of Pride-based products. Ted Butryn's words in 2012 seem just as worthy of consideration today:

> On the surface, the WWE is a shining example of a reformed company looking to "do the right thing" for the country, and while we can applaud the attention to the numerous causes it supports, beneath the veneer of corporate citizenship lies a

wealth of problematic values and business practices. (Butryn
2012: 291)

These problematic values and business practices have been subject to
scrutiny in recent times. Wrestler wellness and the dangers of steroid
abuse were explored in multiple news outlets after the murder-suicide
committed by WWE wrestler Chris Benoit in 2007. The company's
backstage handling of racial abuse has been under scrutiny, with
wrestler Bobby Lashley allegedly leaving WWE in 2008 after racist
comments from a WWE executive went unpunished. WWE's treatment of its wrestlers was also examined on the March 31, 2019
episode of HBO's *Last Week Tonight with John Oliver*, which discussed
the standard wrestling company practice of classing its wrestlers as
independent contractors, as opposed to employees, which means
that they are not entitled to health insurance or retirement benefits
despite being tied to exclusivity deals with WWE. WWE can also be
criticized for its approach to environmental matters, including Daniel
Bryan's 2018–19 presentation as a heel vegan environmentalist. His
opponent, AJ Styles, stood up for the rights of the audience to eat
factory-farmed, mass-produced, hot dogs, and to drive gas-guzzling
SUVs, yet was presented as the hero to Bryan's villain. Here, once
again, we seem to find the mirror held up to just one portion of society, as opposed to the whole, which hinders, rather than aids, social
progress.

Significant questions remain, then, for WWE in terms of whether
it really has adequately responded to and moved on from its racist
and homophobic past. Much as we saw with the case of sexism and
misogyny in the discussion of women's wrestling earlier, there is an
image of progress, but once you look beneath the surface you can see
that problems remain.

4. Commodification and Social Justice

Before we talk more about how pro wrestling companies might act more responsibly in regard to social justice, let's look more closely at questions about whether it is appropriate for them to do so. What if a pro wrestling company decides to be more active and engaged with issues of social justice? What potential pitfalls might we encounter? One issue is that pro wrestling companies are businesses, looking to make money, and would thus profit from successful social justice storylines. Consequently, we can ask if it is wrong for a company to profit from social justice campaigns, and whether this would be a reason to steer clear of them.

To see the potential problems here, we can make a comparison with advertising. Recently, some companies have started to tie social justice projects into their advertising, with mixed results. In 2018 Nike used a picture of Colin Kaepernick, who has been shut out by NFL teams following his anthem protests against police brutality toward African-Americans, with the slogan "Believe in something. Even if it means sacrificing everything." In 2019 Gillette released an advert pondering their "The Best a Man Can Get" slogan in the Me Too era, examining the harms caused by toxic masculinity, and imploring watchers to change their views of what it is to be a man.

These campaigns were powerful, yet controversial. They obviously upset those resistant to the social justice campaigns of the Black Lives Matter and Me Too movements. Regrettably, there are such people – most of them white men – who, perhaps because they feel threatened by such movements, push back hard against them. One risk that companies take in tying their brands to these movements is that they lose customers who oppose the causes, as witnessed by people posting videos of them burning their Nike trainers.

The second, and more serious, layer of controversy concerns the appropriateness of using social justice campaigns in this way. Given the importance of the messages being conveyed, is it appropriate for them to be used to sell products? Despite the fact that it is undoubtedly good for such issues to be considered mainstream, and being in adverts is one way to signify that, the idea of them being co-opted for monetary gain for a particular company adds a degree of uneasiness: it feels a little exploitative. It also heightens concerns about illusory progress: if people start to think that buying the right products is enough to support social justice causes, this will be an obstacle to efforts for real and lasting change.

So, what if a pro wrestling company does decide to consciously include social justice-related storylines in its shows? Is it open to the same criticism that advertising is? Is it monetizing and commodifying something that should not be monetized or commodified? I think the issues here are a little more complex. Undoubtedly, pro wrestling companies are businesses, aimed at making money. However, they are also producing something dramatic. Just like movie studios and TV companies, pro wrestling companies aim to make money, but also produce something of artistic merit. Now, it seems that using social justice issues in an artistic setting is not inappropriate: indeed, it is necessary to disseminate these ideas widely. Movies such as *Get Out*, *Black Panther*, and *BlacKKKlansman*, for example, all amplify the Black Lives Matter movement, and present some of the key ideas in innovative and engaging ways. Even though the studios intend such movies to make money, this does not seem as problematic as the advertising case does. This is because the movies themselves are the ends here; they are not the means by which to persuade someone to buy something else, like a pair of trainers or a razor. Watching the movie and appreciating the art form is the end in itself, and this makes the difference.

So, it seems as though there would be justification for pro wrestling companies to use social justice issues in their storylines in a positive way, on the grounds that it would be in the service of producing an artistic portrayal of the issues to aid understanding, which may also happen to make money, as opposed to simply trying to make money. To put this in the more philosophical terms of the "Doctrine of Double Effect", there is a difference between intending to create art, which, as a side effect, makes money, and just intending to make money. In the former, art – and the message itself – is the goal, and financial reward just something that happens as a result of the art, whereas in the latter, it's just about making money. The idea, according to the Doctrine of Double Effect, is that the difference in intentions makes the actions differ in their moral respectability (with the former being morally permissible, and the latter not), even though the outcomes are the same (money is made).

Now, the issue is complicated somewhat by the fact that pro wrestling companies use their shows to sell products: merchandise sales have always been, and remain, a massive part of the wrestling business, and of wrestlers' income. Again, though, I think that this is different from simply producing commercials for a product. If the merchandise (a T-shirt, say) is connected to something produced for independent artistic merit (a movie, for example), which makes sense as a way of communicating the social justice issues in a meaningful way, then making money as a by-product of that seems justifiable. However, if it is just there to make money, then that seems problematic. We can return to WWE, and their Pride-based products and the "Balor Club is for Everyone" shirt. If these pieces of merchandise are not connected to any meaningful LGBTQ storylines, which use the artistic process to develop social justice issues, this could be seen as just monetization of the LGBTQ rights movement by WWE, and is closer to the moves made by Nike and Gillette to use social justice issues to brand their products. If a company *really* supports LGBTQ rights, and is in a position to do so with their primary product, marketing lucrative special edition T-shirts is not enough to counter silence on the issues in shows and storylines, just like Donald Trump's offering a pro-Pride tweet doesn't make up for his administration's record on LGBTQ rights.

So, pro wrestling companies are in a position where they could present social justice issues in a way that would respect those movements, and aid their success. *Should* they do so? Yes, they should. They present worlds which, although fictional, are very relevant to the struggles real people face in real life, and they should not ignore these struggles, or the movements to forge change.

5. How to be a Socially Responsible Pro Wrestling Company?

Saying this is the easy bit, though. The hard bit is to work out how to do this responsibly. Unfortunately, there are not many examples in pro wrestling history to draw from. One, though is the "Golden Lovers" storyline in New Japan Pro Wrestling, which is in stark contrast to the "Billy and Chuck" storyline in WWE. The storylines are similar in that they both – at some point – feature a tag team with homoerotic overtones, but the ways that these characters and their subsequent development are treated is dramatically different.

The Golden Lovers story features Kenny Omega and Kota Ibushi, and has run over a long period of about 10 years or so, and spans different promotions. It began in the smaller Japanese promotion,

DDT, where Omega and Ibushi started off as rivals. After an intense match between the two, they decided to team up, and formed the tag team known as "Golden Lovers". This team continued into New Japan Pro Wrestling, and the idea that they were more than just tag team partners was heavily implied. Key to this, though, is that the Golden Lovers were not presented as heels. As we have seen, typically in American shows, any character with homosexual overtones is presented as a heel, but this was not the case here, and the Golden Lovers became one of New Japan's most popular teams. When they broke up due to Kenny Omega's heel turn when he joined the Bullet Club, a heel faction of *gaijin*, part of the emotional punch of that turn was the breakup with Ibushi.

The subsequent torment that Omega felt about this was explored subtly throughout the next few years, with one memorable segment being Omega's interference in a match between Ibushi and the Bullet Club leader, AJ Styles. Ibushi, having won the grueling New Japan Cup, had earned an opportunity to fight for New Japan's ultimate prize: the International Wrestling Grand Prix (IWGP) Heavyweight Championship. At ringside with the Bullet Club, Omega had cut a reticent and conflicted figure throughout the match. Just as Ibushi was about to hit his finishing move and win the match, Omega reluctantly distracted him, giving Styles enough time to counter the move, hit his own finisher, and win the match. Styles and the rest of the Bullet Club celebrated as Ibushi lay distraught and sobbing in the ring, his dream destroyed. The conflict within Omega was clear, as he half-heartedly joined in the celebrations with tears in his eyes. The emotion generated by this scene was palpable, with the history between the characters being masterfully brought to bear.

Some time later, Omega kicked AJ Styles out of the Bullet Club, and became its new leader. Ibushi and Omega were kept apart, but then brought back together in dramatic fashion. After losing the IWGP US title, Omega was ousted from the Bullet Club by Cody Rhodes, who, along with the rest of the gang, attacked Omega after his match. As they were about to hit Omega with a steel chair, Ibushi ran in to save him. This left Omega and Ibushi alone in the ring for the first time in years. The tension mounted as Ibushi offered his hand to Omega to help him up, but Omega refused. As the commentators were teasing physical violence, the two passionately embraced. The crowd went crazy, cheering this recon-ciliation, and confetti descended upon the ring. The Golden Lovers then reunited as a tag team, and wrestled more matches together as a team before Omega left New Japan for All Elite Wrestling (AEW) in 2019.

This story continues even when the two are in separate compa-nies. Omega, when asked at the Starrcast II convention in May 2019 whether he'd tried to bring Ibushi to AEW, tearfully said:

I knew that I couldn't ask Ibushi to sign because I knew it was his time, and he deserved it. Anyway, I knew that if I asked for him to come here, that he would. And if I begged for him to come, that he would. But, I knew that his dream before anything that we ever did was to win the IWGP Heavyweight Belt.

There are a number of impressive things about the Golden Lovers storyline. The first is that it takes place over such a long period of time, which is unusual in pro wrestling. For the characters to never forget their history together, even as they are engaged in different feuds and different activities, adds a layer of reality not often seen in pro wrestling storylines. It also spanned different promotions, and dif-ferent media forms, from regular pro wrestling programming to social media and press interviews. As a result, it feels like a *real* relationship, and this is essential to its role as a key LGTBQ storyline. Rather than being presented as caricatures, figures of fun, or threatening heels, an LGBTQ relationship is presented as a real thing, and a precious thing, that fans can not only relate to, but get emotionally invested in. Likewise, the characters are presented as real people, feeling real emotions, as opposed to cartoonish freaks: their LGBTQ identity is key to them, but it is not the *only* relevant thing about them: it is intertwined in their other activities in just the way heterosexual identities are with other performers.

This is one positive case, then, and how might we draw upon it in the future? AEW, founded in 2019, has explicitly stated that it is part of their aims to showcase and celebrate diversity in their shows, and feature openly gay and transgender performers. The AEW Vice President Cody Rhodes was also very open to talking about race when asked about it by Mark Henry in the post *Double Or Nothing* press conference in May 2019. In remarks subsequently praised by US Congresswoman Alexandria Ocasio-Cortez, he said:

> I'm in an interracial marriage, and I've learned a lot I would have never known. I one time told Brandi, "I don't have a racist bone," I said, "I don't see color." And she said "well then you don't see my experience." And I thought "oh, you're right. I can't just say that." You need to be able to see that experience and at least understand it . . . The best wrestlers are gonna field the game and that's a very diverse profile. I'm really proud of it. We're gonna promote them as wrestlers, that's all the elements of diversity. We're not gonna make it a PR element for us. And that I'm really proud of, because it's about the wrestling.

Notice here that Rhodes explicitly says that AEW will not make social justice issues part of their PR, and will aim instead to promote the issues through the wrestling aspect of the business. How might they do this? One line is to try to normalize what may seem to be controversial, such as transgender or gender-neutral performers. This seems to be the line suggested by Sonny Kiss, in an interview with Wrestling Inc's WINCLY podcast:

> I'm just a guy who is feminine, obviously, it's very apparent. But at the same time, I'm just a wrestler and I'm not a "gimmick." I'm just this flamboyant, athletic, flipping dude . . . dude or dudette, however you see it because I'm very ambiguous with my sexuality and gender. I call myself a male but I identify as gender-neutral to the public . . .
>
> People think that they [AEW] are just hiring people due to their sexuality and that's not what they are doing. They are hiring authentic people – transgender and homosexuals as myself – they are hiring people like that to give representation for really good wrestlers and people who don't have that when they look on TV.
>
> People can look on TV and see Nyla and myself and say, "Oh my God! That's someone like me, but not a gimmick." (Transcription from WrestlingInc.com)

Note here Kiss's mention of the idea of authenticity, when he says that, unlike other males who have wrestled as feminine characters, he is the genuine version, as it reflects who he really is outside the ring. This connects back to our discussions of reality and identity in chapters 1 and 3, where we considered the extent to which it matters that the real life of the performer be reflected in their character. In cases pertinent to social justice, such as those of race and sexuality, one could argue that these issues are more acute, as there often is a need to ensure a connection between the performer and the character. We see this in mainstream movies too, where there is a need to align the ethnicity of a character with the actor who plays them. We may think that the same should apply in cases of gender and sexuality too, where there should be more focus on having LGBTQ actors portraying LGBTQ characters, such as when Scarlett Johansson pulled out of playing a transgender man in the movie *Rub & Tug* in 2018.

Kiss also refers to Nyla Rose, who is a trans performer in AEW's women's division. Rose's status as a trans athlete has not been emphasized on AEW shows so far: she has been presented without comment as a performer in the women's division. During her match at *Double Or Nothing*, it was not something that was mentioned at all in the program. When interviewed for Graham Isador's vice.com article in July 2019, Rose said:

Being trans, I don't really have a choice compared to someone gay, les, or bi. People who don't go through any physical changes when being out. My decision to be out as a bisexual, and be open about being trans was intentional. I want others to see the normality in a life that may be different than theirs. I want people to see that there is someone that may be like them thrive and hopefully it can help them find their own courage . . . it may not even be related to anything doing with sexual or gender identity, inspiration comes in many forms.

The fact that a person is allowed to compete in the division of their gender identity without any fanfare or controversy is a remarkable fact in itself when one compares the uproar that such suggestions would cause in sports in general, and, one also presumes, in movies: would the Academy Awards allow a transgender man to be considered for the best actor award? We don't know, but we can be sure that it wouldn't be something that would happen without extensive public scrutiny and discussion.

So, this is certainly one approach: present things as if there is no issue, and allow the performances to speak for themselves. That is, essentially normalize the situation: there are no issues here, and everyone is treated equally *as a wrestler*. This certainly seems to create an inclusive atmosphere where discrimination is not tolerated, and people are treated on their own terms, without intrusive questioning.

This is a positive approach, and AEW is probably the first major pro wrestling company to discuss social justice issues so directly. One does wonder, though, if this is entirely consistent with what Rhodes says above about not being able to ignore race, and that taking a colorblind, or gender-blind, approach does not quite get to the nub of the issue when it comes to issues of social justice. By focusing just on the wrestling attributes of these characters, it certainly seems to suggest that their other features should not be taken to be defining, which is definitely a good thing, and is taking strides toward equal opportunity. However, this may not adequately address the reality of the experiences of minority viewers who do not experience this equality of opportunity in their own lives. Going back to the idea of reflecting the times that we talked about earlier, whilst we may wish to create a non-discriminatory, open environment to hold up as an ideal for how we can treat each other, this may not directly engage with the pressing social issues we all face. By presenting an ideal, and not engaging with the reality, a chance may be missed to be a catalyst for social change.

An alternative direction would be to directly address these issues in storylines, and emphasize the struggles these characters have to overcome just to do what they love, which may push the focus back toward the real struggles that people have in their lives outside of wrestling. However, this also has its drawbacks. For one thing, it places performers in an uncomfortable position, as it may force them to be public about things they do not wish to be public about. It seems unfair to require a performer to address issues in character that are very real to them, and that they may not wish to explore on screen. Indeed, as we noted in chapter 3, it can be tasteless and unfair to explore real-life issues on screen.

Perhaps what's needed is an appropriate blend of approaches that reflects the needs, interests, and creative freedom of the performers. Some performers may want to be more open about the struggles they face, and incorporate them into storylines; whereas others may wish to just avoid tackling them head-on on screen. There may be times when a company feels that there is a need to push an issue on screen that a performer is not entirely comfortable with, and this is a situation that would need as delicate handling – if not more so – as one would find on a movie or TV set when an actor is asked to do something they are not comfortable doing.

Being a socially responsible pro wrestling company is a challenge, and this is just an initial assessment of the importance of thinking about how to manage both the desire for equal opportunity and the need to not ignore important issues. It's one of the most important issues to think about in pro wrestling, particularly given the genre's troubled history with racism, homophobia, and sexism. This history still tarnishes pro wrestling's public image, and finding ways to make genuine and lasting improvements are important steps for pro wrestling to take.

6

Meaning: Sport vs Monster

We've talked a lot about pro wrestling, but haven't really tackled the question of what pro wrestling actually is head on. It's time to do that now. This is a difficult question, even for those who are deeply interested or involved in it. Is it a sport? Or "sports entertainment", as WWE likes to present it? We'll see that the issue of whether pro wrestling is a sport is more complex than we might think, and that it is surprisingly difficult to rule out pro wrestling as a sport. We'll also see that there are significant questions over whether the term "sports entertainment" is at all helpful when it comes to categorizing pro wrestling. Finally, we'll look at whether pro wrestling is something that, by nature, resists characterization – a "monster" – and what this tells us about both pro wrestling and ourselves.

1. Philosophy and Definition

Philosophers are suckers for a good definition. Ever since Socrates demanded an account of what piety is in Plato's dialogue *Euthyphro*, the quest for clear and precise definitions has been part and parcel of philosophical work. In *Euthyphro*, the character Euthyphro claims to know the nature of piety, which prompts Socrates to ask him detailed questions about it. Socrates points out the distinction between just naming things that are pious, and saying what piety *is*, i.e. what all and only pious things have in common, which Euthyphro tries to do, without much success. Socrates's question drives much of philosophical inquiry into the essence of things, and, whilst it hasn't always ended in any great philosophical success, engaging in this process is a way of clarifying thought, and digging into the key issues surrounding something. Pro wrestling provides an interesting case to get stuck into questions of definition, as it seems stubbornly resistant to any clear categorization: is it a sport? Not quite. Is it entertainment? Sort of, but this doesn't capture it fully. Is it "sports entertainment"? Maybe, but what the hell does that mean?! In this chapter we'll examine these questions in more detail.

2. Pro Wrestling as Sport

Many times in the 1990s, WCW viewers were treated to announcer Tony Schiavone saying "This is the greatest night in the history of our sport." And, for many years, pro wrestling was presented as a sport. To suggest otherwise would be to break kayfabe and traitorously reveal the industry's secrets, an offense similar in magnitude to the breaking of the magician's code. The first major pro wrestling promoter to publicly state that pro wrestling is not a sport was Vince McMahon, owner of the WWF in 1989. McMahon did this for financial reasons, to avoid paying state athletic commission fees. Moreover, as noted below, by stating that pro wrestling was not a sport, and rather, "sports entertainment", the WWF was able to rebrand the product and engage fans (and advertisers) in a new way.

However, watching the shows themselves, pro wrestling continues to present itself as a sport today, even though it is generally accepted that all involved know otherwise, aside from the youngest viewers. The action is presented as a physical contest for supremacy, with referees, rules, winners, and losers. There are champions, championship matches, and tournaments. The announcers call the action like a sport: they discuss what the competitor's strategies are, their records against their opponents, and how they might get out of certain problematic situations. Sometimes there is a "tale of the tape" shown on screen beforehand, comparing the various attributes and accolades of the participants. Wrestlers are overjoyed when they win; despondent when they lose. Those who win matches get opportunities, and those who lose try to avoid a losing streak. Some wrestling companies, such as New Japan Pro Wrestling, which brands itself as "King of Sports", stick closer to a sport-based presentation than others, such as WWE. WWE is more storyline driven, focusing on developing personal animosity between wrestlers to hype a match, whereas New Japan typically focuses more on tournaments and mimicking genuine athletic competition, where there is an in-built reason for animosity between opponents, namely that they want to be the best.

Either way, though, now that kayfabe is dead, almost everyone knows that this presentation is just that – presentation. There is no genuine contest *to win the match*, as this is something that is decided by the bookers, not by the unfolding of the contest in the ring. As Roland Barthes puts it in his famous essay "The World of Wrestling", "the function of the wrestler is not to win; it is to go exactly through the motions that are expected of him" (Barthes 1972: 16). Champions are booked to be champions, tournament winners are booked to win the tournaments, and the announcers' comments on the respective strengths and weaknesses of the combatants is purely there to supplement the action for dramatic effect, even if they are based on their apparent physical characteristics.

But, does this alone mean that it is not a sport? It seems so, but to be sure we need to have some grip on what a sport is. We also need to think more carefully about what sorts of sports pro wrestling is most like, which, I suggest, may surprisingly not be amateur wrestling, boxing, or other combat sports.

2.1 Refereed Sports and Performance Sports

One clear obstacle to thinking of pro wrestling as a sport is that there is not a genuine contest going on in the ring during a pro wrestling match. These are precisely the grounds used by Allen Guttmann to rule out pro wrestling as a sport. Guttmann, following Barthes, places pro wrestling as an art form, as opposed to a sport, on the grounds that a pro wrestling match is not a genuine contest:

> The activity engaged in by professional wrestlers looks somewhat like the activity of college wrestlers, but the feigned struggle is not really a contest. It is rather a kind of folk-art, a melodramatic allegory of good and evil. (Guttmann 1978: 12)

Now, we cannot dispute that – in nearly all cases – pro wrestling matches are not genuine contests in the way that amateur wrestling matches are. However, does this show that pro wrestling is not a sport? I think not; I think at most it shows that pro wrestling is not a sport like amateur wrestling, but these considerations remain silent on whether pro wrestling is a sport of a different kind.

The philosopher Bernard Suits (1988) draws a distinction between refereed sports and performance sports. Think of the difference, for example, between soccer and gymnastics. In soccer you have two teams aiming to achieve a particular goal, and a referee there to mediate the activity. Ideally, mediating is all the referee needs to do: *the teams* ultimately decide who wins, with the referee just there to make sure nothing goes awry. In gymnastics, though, the referees, or judges, play a much more involved role. It is *their judgments*, through their scores, that decide who wins, even though those judgments are made on the basis of the performances of the athletes involved.

If we accept this as a distinction between sports, then I think we have a way to conceive of pro wrestling as a genuine sport. My suggestion will be that we think of pro wrestling not as a sport in the way that amateur wrestling, boxing, or MMA are sports, but in the way that gymnastics, synchronized swimming, diving, and figure skating are sports.

Think about gymnastics for example, particularly floor routines. These are pre-planned, practiced routines, where the gymnast is expected to perform a set of moves established by their training routine. It is observed as an athletic performance of these moves, and is judged by how well the gymnast performs the routine. Here we have an example of something that is pre-determined, in that the routine is set in advance, and is athletic, yet it is classed as a sport, and, moreover, an Olympic sport. The same applies for other sports, such as synchronized swimming, diving, and figure skating. In each of these cases, an athlete – or a pair of athletes – has a set routine that they must perform, and the key expectation of the activity is that they perform this routine to perfection.

The proper question, then, is whether pro wrestling can be considered a sport in this sense, as these sports seem to be closer to the sort of activities that pro wrestlers engage in during a match. One issue is that, at least as it appears, there are no judges holding up scorecards after each match, and that such a process does not determine the winners as presented. However, there is a significant aspect of pro wrestling analysis that formalizes the idea of judging performance, namely the "star ratings" offered by influential newsletters like the *Wrestling Observer Newsletter* and *Pro Wrestling Torch*. These systems rank pro wrestling matches out of five stars (though six stars have been awarded, as have negative stars). Awards are given by these publications for the best matches of the year, and some pro wrestlers specifically acknowledge their success in these awards in their on-screen personas, such as Kenny Omega's presentation as "The Best Bout Machine". Note here that what is claimed of Omega is not that he *wins* matches, but that he provides *the best* matches.

Another example is the presentation of CM Punk as "the best in the world". This was not given as a claim to be able to beat anyone, but a claim to be the best wrestler, capable of putting on the best matches. This was pitched in contrast to Punk's rival at the time, John Cena, who many fans felt was not a good wrestler, despite his winning a vast number of matches and titles. Cena's responses to Punk's claim to be the best was to list the people he had beaten, but, as many fans pointed out, this was to miss the point of what Punk was saying, and to engage in a different conversation.

This sort of competition was formalized in WCW for a brief time in the late 1980s, where a financial bonus was awarded to the wrestlers that were judged to have had the best match of the night. But this general form of competition is there between all wrestlers to be the best at what they do. This level of competition is intense, and pro wrestling is just as competitive as anything else – if not more so – when it comes to competition for the top spot in a company. This is based not on who can win a match in a genuine fight, but who the best performer is, both in the ring and on the mic. Equipped with these thoughts about pro wrestling criticism, and even formalized competition when it comes to putting on the best matches, the case could be made that pro wrestling is a sport in the same sense that gymnastics is.

However, one could say that, whilst this level of performance and criticism is important, nevertheless the *primary* goal of a pro wrestling match is to entertain, not to provide a great match from a technical standpoint. To return to the Doctrine of Double Effect that we talked about in the previous chapter, the difference between the gymnast and the pro wrestler is that the gymnast's primary goal is to display athletic excellence for the benefit of the judges, not to entertain the audience, which is a by-product of the activity. The primary goal of the pro wrestler, on the other hand, is to entertain the audience, and if they do so by way of displaying a high degree of technical ability for the benefit of those evaluating, so be it, but this is a by-product of the main aim, which is to entertain.

Evaluating this idea, however, is tricky. Undoubtedly, from the point of view of the pro wrestling promoter, or company, the primary goal is to entertain, as this will attract more viewers, and more ticket holders, to the product. But can we say with assurance that this is the goal of the pro wrestlers themselves? This seems like a stretch, and not just because figuring out an individual's motivation is tricky in general. Perhaps some pro wrestlers *are* more concerned with the execution of the match as a great pro wrestling match, and feel that the audience's enjoyment flows from that. In other words, maybe pro wrestlers see themselves as aiming to perfect the activity of pro wrestling, and that entertainment is a by-product of this, just as the gymnast sees themselves as aiming to perfect the floor routine, and thinking that entertainment will follow for those that appreciate it.

In comparing pro wrestling to these more performance-based sports, it seems harder to make the distinction between sports and entertainment. Many of these routines carry elements of storytelling, emotion, and character development, in addition to being feats of athletic accomplishment (think, for example, of figure skaters Torville and Dean's legendary "Bolero" routine). Consider also how the gymnast Katelyn Ohashi's perfect 10 floor routine went viral in 2019. When you watch this routine, and the reactions from the crowd, the lines between gymnastics and pro wrestling become increasingly blurred. One can imagine pro wrestling being an Olympic sport in this way, where pairs of pro wrestlers enact matches that are judged by experts for technical skill.

My proposal here, then, is not that pro wrestling *must* be considered a sport, but rather that, once we explore the ways it resembles various sports, there is a reasonable case to be made that it could be considered a sport. If someone is dead-set on holding that it is not a sport in any sense, then in my view they need to demonstrate what exactly it is that distinguishes pro wrestling not from boxing or amateur wrestling, but from gymnastics, figure skating, diving, synchronized swimming, and other performance-based sports.

To this end, though, there is much to say. I have suggested that there are sufficient similarities between pro wrestling and performance-based sports to yield the idea that pro wrestling is a sport. One might wonder, though, whether this leads to the category of performance-based sports being too broad, and including things that we would not want to class as sports. Take ballet, for example. This is an activity that requires a high level of athletic proficiency and skill; it involves performing a set routine; and has theatrical, story-telling aspects. It is also an activity that is not formally judged in the way that figure skating and gymnastics are, but it is an activity that is judged in other ways, for example by theatre reviews and dance aficionados. The same may extend to certain forms of musical performance: certain instruments require a degree of physical exertion to play, and the level of theatricality demanded at a stadium rock concert, for example, may place a significant physical demand on a performer. Whilst pro wrestling companies frequently say "this ain't ballet", if what has been said above is correct, it starts to be harder to see the difference!

Once again, the issues here may boil down to the idea of a contest. The performance-based sports like gymnastics and figure skating are cases where we have competitors directly competing against one another to win the judges' best score, and the scoring of the judges is a direct part of the activity as it is practiced. The judges do not operate at a "once-removed" level of critical analysis or evaluation; rather the judges' scores are part of the activity, and determine those who win "from the inside", as it were. The ideas of scoring and evaluation in pro wrestling and ballet, however, come from a place outside the activity itself – from enthusiasts who appreciate the performance, and subject it to their own, independent, critical observations.

If we take this view, then whilst pro wrestling and ballet are not sports, it would not take much for them to turn into sports. If judges were introduced into the activity, and pro wrestling matches or ballet performances were put on by competing groups of individuals specifically to obtain high scores from the judges, then they could be considered sports.

But wait! Have we not now opened a new can of worms? What about TV shows like Strictly Come Dancing, or Dancing With the Stars, or even Top Chef? Here we have shows where contestants do exactly this! They put on a performance specifically to obtain scores from the judges. Does our analysis now mean that these are sports, in just the same way that gymnastics and figure skating are? Or, perhaps, does this show – as the philosopher Ludwig Wittgenstein (1953) famously explored with games – that sport is not something we can really define at all?

There is one key thing to bear in mind here, though, which is that sport is a category loaded with social and institutional baggage. One key difference between Olympic sports and TV shows like Strictly Come Dancing is that the former are regulated by a particular institutional body – the International Olympic Committee in this case – whereas the latter are not. Contests run by television companies only have to answer to the television networks themselves when it comes to setting up the rules for competition and competitor eligibility. Contests run as sporting contests, however, have to answer to specific institutional governing bodies who dictate what the rules are, and what people are eligible to compete. This is a key difference between the game of kicking a ball around a field, and the sport of Premier League soccer. Sport, in other words, is an institutionally loaded category in that, to be a sport, an activity has to be regulated in a particular way by a particular kind of institution.

As a consequence, even though TV shows like Strictly Come Dancing, Dancing With the Stars, or Top Chef involve people engaging in competitive activity and being judged on their performance, because they are run by TV studios, and not regulated by a recognized sporting institutional body, they are not sports, even if they share some features in common with them. This also gives us further grounds to rule out ballet and pro wrestling as sports, even though they share features in common with performance-based sports: because they are not run and regulated by sporting institutions, they are not sports. Once again, though, it would not take a great deal to change this status, and what would change would be the establishment of a particular institutional body that would provide the necessary regulations and guidelines on competition and eligibility, and clearly set out the necessary procedures for judges to follow.

So, the takeaway here is that the issue of whether or not pro wrestling is a sport is a lot more nuanced than it is generally taken to be, but there remain substantial grounds to deny that pro wrestling is a sport. If it is not a sport, though, then what is it: "sports entertainment"? It is to this idea that we turn next.

3. Pro Wrestling as Sports Entertainment

As noted above, it was the WWF who first moved from using the term "sport" to describe pro wrestling, to the term "sports entertainment". We noted that it was partly to avoid having to pay state athletic commission fees, but it was also a new way to market the product to advertisers, as Stephanie McMahon explained in a speech at the WWE Business Partner Summit in 2018:

> Advertisers either had an adverse reaction to the words "professional wrestling," or they simply didn't understand what it was. So, how could we create a term or a label that potential partners could understand? How could we describe that WWE was based on larger-than-life characters enthralled in relatable storylines? That was when we coined the term "sports entertainment".

The question for us, though, is not whether the term "sports entertainment" is useful to avoid fees, or attract advertisers, but rather whether it is useful as a way to define what pro wrestling is, or even a useful category at all.

A first point to consider is whether the term "sports entertainment" really makes sense. After all, one might wonder, aren't all sports entertainment of a sort? Many people watch sports precisely to be entertained, and this is what dictates the success or otherwise of a sport. Sports that people stop watching (like roller derby) end up ceasing to exist, as most of the money that pays players and participants comes from people paying to watch it. In this sense, all professional sport, at least nowadays, cannot escape the idea that sports are a form of entertainment, and their survival depends on it. Indeed, many sports change their formulae precisely in an effort to be more entertaining, and attract more viewers, as has been witnessed in recent years with Barry Hearn's efforts to popularize and develop the appeal of snooker, and cricket's turn to short-form Twenty20 games (funnily enough, some of these changes, such as giving entrance music for players, are taken straight from pro wrestling!). Similarly, Sky Sports' launch of the Premier League transformed the way soccer was presented on television, and in pretty much every sporting presentation a lot of effort goes into making the event as entertaining as possible for the viewer, even sometimes at the expense of the players.

Despite this, one could point out that professional sport is just one form of sport, and that, as the philosopher Kendall Walton (2015) argues, the *primary goal* of sports is not to entertain, but that this is a by-product: sports *happen* to entertain, but their *purpose* is not to entertain. Sports can thus be played "behind closed doors", or without any audience at all, and this does not affect the nature of the activity. "Sports entertainment", on the other hand, is different.

Drawing on some of the thoughts expressed earlier, though, one could argue that there is a primary goal of pro wrestling that is not to entertain, which is to perfect the activity of pro wrestling – displaying one's skill at the various components that make for an excellent pro wrestler and pro wrestling match. This can also be carried out without an audience, or without a need to entertain – we can imagine two pro wrestlers just having a match on their own with the aim of having the best match possible. In contrast to this, we might think that the components of a great pro wrestling match are essentially dramatic: building a story, eliciting emotions from the crowd, building suspense, and developing a satisfying conclusion. Even a match conducted "behind closed doors" will still be constructed with these things in mind – for an imaginary audience, if you will. As the philosopher Lisa Jones (2019) argues, pro wrestling, perhaps more than any other form of entertainment, gives the audience an essential role to play.

Whatever our views on this issue, we might still think that "sports entertainment" is too broad a term to define pro wrestling. Think of the movie *Escape to Victory*, for example, where Allied prisoners of war in World War II play a soccer match against a German team which leads to their escape. This involves portrayal of a sport – soccer – and the primary goal is to entertain. Likewise, movies like *The Karate Kid*, *Bend it Like Beckham*, and *Invictus*: these all involve sporting activity where the aim is to entertain, not compete. From a different direction, we have TV shows such as *Gladiators*, or *American Ninja Warrior*, where there is genuine competition between contestants, but the primary aim of the activity is still to entertain. (Think of the peculiarity of a *Gladiators* contest held behind closed doors.)

So, whilst we can distinguish pro wrestling from other sports by thinking about the aim of the activity being entertainment (and hence the term "sports entertainment"), this doesn't help us distinguish pro wrestling from other forms of sports entertainment. To do this, we really need to do what WWE seems to want to get away from, and recognize that the "wrestling" aspect of "pro wrestling" is an essential part of what it is. The way to distinguish pro wrestling from other forms of sports entertainment is by examining the sport it originates from. There is no doubt that pro wrestling grew out of what we now call amateur wrestling, in its various forms. The idea of worked matches grew out of what were originally shoot matches.

Wrestling holds and moves previously used in genuine athletic contests were co-opted for the purposes of producing an entertaining, worked, product.

What this suggests is that it is hard to keep the "wrestling" out of "pro wrestling". Even if we buy into the notion of sports entertainment, we still need to use the term "wrestling" to clarify what sport is relevant for the entertaining. So, it is a mistake to say that pro wrestling is just sports entertainment. It is a form of sports entertainment, at most. This still leaves open the question of what pro wrestling itself is.

The challenge of categorizing pro wrestling thus proves tricky. But perhaps it is supposed to, because pro wrestling is precisely the sort of thing that resists categorization. Let's look at this idea now.

4. Pro Wrestling as a Monster

There is a powerful thought that pro wrestling, by its very nature, is something that resists definition. Henry Jenkins III, for example, draws upon the work of Jeffrey Cohen (1996) on monsters to suggest that pro wrestling is something that is monstrous in that it cannot clearly fit into any pre-existing category. Here is Jenkins talking about WWE:

> The WWE is a horrifying hybrid-not sports, sports entertainment; not real, not fake, but someplace in between; appealing to the "white trash" working class and the college educated alike; courting kids and appealing to adolescents on the basis of its rejection of family values; existing outside the cultural mainstream and yet a commercial success; appealing to national pride

even as it shoots a bird at most American institutions; masculine as hell and melodramatic as all get out. (Jenkins 2005: 299)

Of course, some of the things Jenkins says are specifically aimed at WWE, but many of the points apply to pro wrestling in general. Let's talk for a moment about Cohen's idea of a monster, and how it relates to pro wrestling.

4.1 What are Monsters?

Cohen says of monsters:

[The] refusal to participate in the classificatory "order of things" is true of monsters generally: they are disturbing hybrids whose externally incoherent bodies resist attempts to include them in any systematic structuration. And so the monster is dangerous, a form suspended between forms that threatens to smash distinctions. (Cohen 1996: 6)

Cohen is initially thinking of monsters like Frankenstein's monster, for example, that take some particular physical form, which is hard to categorize. Frankenstein's monster is a human-like "creature" created by a scientist, Dr Frankenstein, who has a number of human-like qualities. The question of whether the monster is human, though, is a vexed one, and this is part of the point of the story. Other monsters like zombies, werewolves, and vampires fit into this pattern: they bear sufficient similarities to human beings to at least raise the question of whether they are human or not, and part of their appeal is that these questions do not have obvious answers.

Part of the essence of monsters, Cohen thinks, is that their "unnatural" state disrupts the neat and natural ways we categorize things in the world. We have, we think, a neat and natural distinction between living things and dead things. A zombie disrupts this distinction; part of what makes it monstrous is that we can't find a place for it within our normal categories.

Now, whilst Cohen is primarily talking about creatures that take some particular physical form, as Jenkins suggests, we can apply these ideas to cultural phenomena as well. These ideas seem to clearly resonate with pro wrestling. As we have seen, it is something that is difficult to categorize, and that fits uncomfortably into general cultural distinctions. We think we have nice and neat categories that distinguish sport from entertainment, but pro wrestling is monstrous in that it disrupts these categories. It is part sport, part entertainment – but neither completely. This makes it an outsider, incapable of being accepted by more traditional forms of cultural appreciation. Its resistance to categorization also makes it somewhat of an embarrassment: no-one can work out quite what it's supposed to be, and many steer clear of it. As Guy Evans discusses in his book *Nitro* (2018), this significantly affected WCW, who were owned by a television company – Turner Broadcasting – as most of the executives in Turner Broadcasting, aside from Ted Turner himself, didn't understand pro wrestling and saw it as an embarrassment to the company.

This monstrous existence reflects pro wrestling's status as a perennial outsider in regard to popular culture more generally. Just like a monster who is shut out of regular society, pro wrestling seems unable to fully break into mainstream media in the way that other forms of entertainment can. There are moments – sometimes you see sports players using wrestling poses in celebrations, and the occasional catchphrase sneaks through, but not often, and rarely does everyone realize that its origin is pro wrestling. Also, just like a monster, pro wrestling often craves this mainstream acceptance. WWE, for example, is always trying everything it can to be recognized (e.g. by having celebrities at WrestleMania; features on ESPN and HBO), but it is never fully accepted. As a result, it created its own "universe" ("the WWE universe", which is often mentioned on its shows) where it can comfortably live; a world with its own rules and history. When mainstream folks enter it, they are immediately given preference over the wrestlers, who are second best in terms of fame and significance. Perhaps its "monstrous" state is why it is largely ignored by the mainstream, hidden away in the basement and left alone.

4.2 Pro Wrestling's Monstrous Origin

Why would pro wrestling take this monstrous form? Cohen says of the origin of monsters:

> The monster is born . . . as an embodiment of a certain cultural moment – of a time, a feeling, and a place. The monster's body quite literally incorporates fear, desire, anxiety, and fantasy (ataractic or incendiary), giving them life and an uncanny independence. The monstrous body is pure culture. A construct and projection, the monster exists only to be read: the *monstrum* is etymologically "that which reveals", "that which warns", a glyph that seeks a hierophant. (Cohen 1996: 4)

We can take a look at pro wrestling's origins, which are in the bizarre world of the carnival and the circus. This was even acknowledged as recently as March 2019, when the WWE Raw Women's Champion, Ronda Rousey, presenting herself as a "real" MMA fighter, called her WrestleMania 35 opponents Becky Lynch and Charlotte Flair "carnie con artists" on the March 11 episode of Raw. Carnivals already had a part in the monstrous with their "freak shows" that promised curious observers sights of monstrous hybrid creatures. As Scott Beekman (2006) describes, the pro wrestling that we know today began as part of a carnival attraction. With regular amateur wrestling dwindling in popularity, new methods were employed to attract attention. Carnivals would set up challenges where an audience member could take on their featured wrestler, and win a cash prize if they lasted for a certain amount of time in the ring with them. In order to stir up interest, a second wrestler would be planted in the crowd as an audience member, who would take on the champion, and lose after a lengthy and spirited display. The idea was that this would encourage regular audience members to take on the challenge, who would then be quickly dispatched. Worked wrestling matches thus began as a kind of hustle, with their presentation as real matches being designed to make others believe that they could last with the champion.

Promoters began to realize that putting on worked matches could constitute an attraction in itself. The problem with traditional amateur wrestling was that it had become not particularly interesting to watch, but this could be remedied by having the wrestlers work together to put on a show, as opposed to working against each other to try to win. The transition from real competition to worked matches was gradual, and the fact that some matches were worked was a closely guarded secret. But wrestling's transition from amateur to pro really constituted a substantial change in the nature of the activity: it had *mutated* from genuine sport to athletic theatre. Moreover, this mutation seemed necessary for its survival. It was necessary for the survival of wrestling as an attraction, and for the ability of wrestlers to continue to earn their livelihood. Much as the survival of living creatures relies on genetic mutations that suit their environment, the survival of wrestling relied on mutating its form in order to suit its audience.

4.3 Pro Wrestling: the Monster and Us

If we think of pro wrestling as a monster, with its origins in mutation from amateur wrestling in carnival settings, what else can this tell us? In particular, what can it tell us about the creators of this monster, namely ourselves? Cohen has much to say on this issue in general:

> Monsters are our children. They can be pushed to the farthest margins of geography and discourse, hidden away at the edges of the world and in the forbidden recesses of our mind, but they always return. And when they come back, they bring not just a fuller knowledge of our place in history and the history of knowing our place, but they bear self-knowledge, *human* knowledge – and a discourse all the more sacred as it arises from the Outside. These monsters ask us how we perceive the world, and how we have misrepresented what we have attempted to place. They ask us to reevaluate our cultural assumptions about race, gender, sexuality, our perception of difference, our tolerance toward its expression. They ask us why we have created them. (Cohen 1996: 20)

Pro wrestling, perhaps more than any other form of entertainment, prompts this "why" question: *Why* do you watch that? *Why* is it enjoyable? The monstrous state of pro wrestling is apparent here, as none of these questions are asked to watchers of more conventionally categorized shows like sporting events or TV series. Nobody says to avid *Game of Thrones* fans, "you know it's not real, right? There aren't *really* any dragons", just as few people question the appeal of watching sports like basketball and soccer. Pro wrestling fans encounter this skepticism more than watchers of other shows, maybe because of pro wrestling's refusal to be categorized in conventional terms.

Setting aside kids who think that pro wrestling is real competition, the question of "why do you watch that?" is often posed to adults who watch pro wrestling. Indeed, there is often bewilderment expressed: "you know they're not *really* fighting, right?". The difficulty of answering this question makes pro wrestling seem somewhat shameful to enjoy: it's seen as a guilty pleasure, and many people (myself included, in the past) would hide their enjoyment of it. Pro wrestling contains within it a challenge of sorts: Why are you watching this? How do you perceive what's going on? Why do you find it interesting? This fits with Cohen's idea of monsters as containing a challenge by their very existence: Why am I here? Why did you make me like this? What does my existence say about *you*?

These are important questions, and if you've been paying attention, this book gives you a whole lot of answers to them. Pro wrestling is fascinating because it confronts us with issues central to human life. It pushes us to think about reality, and how the way things appear to us might not be the way they really are. It forces us to think about the extent to which we are free in our lives, and about who we really are as individuals. It asks us to consider what makes a person good or bad, and how we can implement that in our lives. It can – if done right – be a force for social change, and – if done wrong – dangerously contribute to deep problems in our society. It can force us to think about categories that seem obvious, but are all the more complex when we think about them more. And that is the key: it makes us laugh, it makes us cry, it makes us cheer, it makes us boo. But, crucially, it can also make us think, discuss, criticize, analyse, debate, and pursue truth about issues fundamental to what it is to be human. It can make us *philosophers*.

Dark Match:

Pro Wrestling vs Philosophy

I hope you now have a sense of some of the philosophical aspects of pro wrestling. I want to close the show by reversing this, and talking about the pro wrestling of philosophy. If you've always wanted to know more about philosophy and what philosophers do but weren't sure where to start, this is for you! If you're already well-acquainted with philosophy, buckle up, as Socrates has a lot more in common with Stone Cold Steve Austin than you might think!

1. Philosophy and Wrestling

Trying to state exactly what philosophy is is a tricky task. In general, philosophers ask fundamental questions about the nature of reality, and the nature of what it is to be a human being, and live a human life. Classic philosophical questions include: Is reality independent of our perceptions of it? What is truth? Do we know anything? What is it to be a person? What is the good life, and how does one live it? How should we act toward one another? How should a good state be organized?

At least on paper, philosophers aim to discover answers to these questions. The philosophical method proceeds by stating, analyzing, defending, and critiquing *arguments*. Philosophical inquiry requires one to state a position, and then defend that position using reasoned arguments. Arguments here are not the shouting matches that occur when someone cuts in line at the grocery store, but structures of statements and reasons for those statements that are given in support.

The back-and-forth nature of philosophical method invites comparisons with combat of various sorts (more on the drawbacks of this comparison below). Wrestling is one example of a combat sport that has invited comparisons with philosophy. Indeed, the Ancient Greek philosopher Protagoras even called his book on truth *The Throws*, to emphasize that his back-and-forth argumentative style mimicked the grappling in a wrestling match. Philosophy students in Ancient Greece were also required to supplement their studies with physical activities such as wrestling. Skillful philosophical argument seems to require the same sorts of imaginative abilities that a combat fighter needs in order to identify the weaknesses of their opponent, as well as their own, and adapt their position as required.

Of course, this is what we would nowadays call amateur wrestling, which is a different activity from pro wrestling. Let's now talk about that.

2. Narrative Structures

Pro wrestling matches are intended to tell stories, as opposed to be genuine athletic contests. Philosophical works also tell stories of their own: they tell the story of why the author's view is the one that should be accepted. Some works of philosophy are more explicitly put in this narrative form, such as the dialogues of the Ancient Greek philosopher Plato.

2.1 Plato's Dialogues

Plato wrote most of his philosophy as dialogues – staged battles, in effect – where his main character Socrates would take on all-comers in the arena of philosophical debate. When one reads one of Plato's dialogues, one knows that the outcome is pre-determined (in almost every case, Socrates wins the argument!), and one knows that the narrative is structured in such a way as to give Socrates worthy opponents who can give him a significant challenge to overcome. This mirrors very closely the typical narrative of a wrestling match, particularly when one compares Plato's Socratic dialogues to the runs of Hulk Hogan in the 1980s, or John Cena in the 2000s. In these cases, it was inevitable that Hogan or Cena would win; the question was how they would overcome the challenges put in their way.

To demonstrate this, we can re-describe Plato's dialogues as pro wrestling matches, and see that the narrative structure of the debate can be expressed in terms of the moves in a wrestling match.

Consider Plato's dialogue *Phaedo*. This is a dialogue about death, and involves Socrates discussing with his friends Simmias and Cebes the question of whether we should fear death. Simmias and Cebes are convinced that Socrates should be afraid of dying, and Socrates is constantly fighting against this idea, through a number of different arguments. In this we can see the character Socrates as the babyface, and Simmias and Cebes as the heels (although they are very friendly). In the initial exchanges we see the strength of the babyface by having Socrates win some initial skirmishes. Simmias and Cebes then pose a challenge much more serious than any faced so far, which leads to a moment of calm and uncertainty, where neither side seems to know what to do. After some digression, Socrates launches his comeback, responds to the objection, and wins the argument. Of course, he dies at the end of the dialogue, but that doesn't mean he didn't win.

You can imagine this as a wrestling match, with Socrates taking on both Simmias and Cebes in a 2-on-1 handicap match. First of all, Socrates shows his prowess by beating them both up, forcing them to keep tagging in and out. For every move they try, he has a counter. They land a couple of minor blows, but Socrates is never really in any danger. Then, suddenly, they team up and hit Socrates with a devastating double team move that leaves him floored and winded. He rolls out of the ring to collect himself, occasionally rolling back in and out to break the referee's ten count. Simmias and Cebes – as they are not *vicious* heels – remain in the ring waiting for Socrates to come back in. Eventually he crawls back in, shakes his head clear, and readies himself for the final battle. We join the announce team: "Right hand to Simmias, right hand to Cebes. Right hand to Simmias, right hand to Cebes. The crowd is going wild! He just . . . he just clotheslined Simmias right out of the ring! Suplex to Cebes, piledriver to Cebes. What a maneuver! Pin, hooks the leg, 1-2-3. He got him! He got him! Socrates wins!".

Think also of Plato's dialogue *Euthyphro*, where a headstrong young Euthyphro, convinced of the correctness of his views about the nature of piety, encounters Socrates who systematically dismantles them until Euthyphro decides he has somewhere else to be and leaves. We could re-describe this as follows.

Euthyphro comes down the aisle, head held high, chest puffed out. "He clearly thinks a lot of himself", says the commentator, as he juts his jaw out confidently and disparagingly toward the crowd. Socrates waits in the ring, the grizzled veteran, much like the legendary Stu Hart, his slight and crooked frame paling in comparison to Euthyphro's chiseled physique. Euthyphro enters the ring and poses for the crowd, drawing a chorus of boos. The bell rings; they lock up.

Euthyphro tries to overpower Socrates, but finds that, every time he tries, Socrates is able to twist his arm into an uncomfortable hold. Frustrated, Euthyphro tries to tackle Socrates, but Socrates counters with a headlock and holds him to the mat. As he releases him, Socrates utters a chuckle. Euthyphro bounces off the ropes, and aims a massive clothesline at Socrates, but Socrates grabs his arm and twists him down to the mat in an armbar. Euthyphro slaps the mat in frustration. Socrates releases Euthyphro, who then walks out the ring down the aisle to the back, swearing and gesticulating to jeers all the way. Socrates stands in the ring, looks at the crowd, and just shrugs.

2.2 General Narratives

Now, whilst not all philosophy is written in dialogues – in fact, most of it is not – the narrative structure of a philosophical work typically retains the same elements. In a philosophy paper one is arguing a point, and this usually involves either critiquing an opponent, or defending your view from an opponent, or both. For this to work, one needs to build one's opponent up as a worthy adversary, make clear the challenge presented, and then show how it can be overcome.

Pro wrestling matches too tend to have a standard formula, though, of course, this does not mean that there are not deviations from it. One such formula is memorably described by the pro wrestler turned trainer Al Snow, who described what he called the "Seven Deadly Steps" on an episode of the *Steve Austin Show* podcast:

Al Snow's "Seven Deadly Steps":

1. Babyface Shine – At the start of the match, the babyface must show some fire by looking good doing a few moves to the heel.

2. The Heat Spot – The heel cuts the babyface's offense off with some big impressive moves.

3. Extensive Heel Beatdown.

4. The Hope Spot – The babyface keeps trying to come back, and looks like they're about to do it, but the heel keeps cutting them off.

5. The Double Down – Both wrestlers hit each other simultaneously, and are down selling for a while.

6. The Comeback – The babyface fights back against the heel, who will stop defending themselves.

7. The Finish/False Finishes – Each wrestler tries to pin the other, in a series of dramatically close pinfall attempts.

Whilst given tongue-in-cheek, Snow's steps describe a narrative progression through a match that is designed to maximize the crowd's reaction to the babyface and heel characters. The babyface is able to show fire and energy, the heel looks vicious and dominating, the babyface fights back against the odds, and the match is excitingly close until a winner is declared. In doing this, we give the babyface and the heel the best chance to "get over" (get their intended crowd reactions) by showcasing their characters and their strengths.

When writing a philosophical work, obviously the author's intentions are different from Snow's in describing the model of a match: a philosopher wants to persuade the reader of their conclusion, as opposed to getting two characters over. However, closer examination reveals that what the philosopher is after is not that different. Typically, when one is arguing for a view, one has to show why it is a better view than a competitor's, or how it can respond to objections raised by an opponent. Indeed, this is part of the combative aspects of philosophical argument that we discussed earlier. To get the reader interested, though, the author has to hook them by showing what is at stake here: they have to draw them in to get them interested.

Once they have done that, they need to keep things interesting by showing that the author's view has some obstacles to overcome, in the form of objections posed. The stronger these objections look, the bigger the author's achievement in overcoming them, so they have a vested interest in making their opponents look strong. The author thus needs to accomplish a number of things: they need to make their view look interesting enough to want to support; they have to show that there are significant problems it needs to overcome, though; and they need to show how these obstacles can be overcome. If they want to up the ante, they can solve some initial problems and then show how these problems lead to bigger problems that they then aim to overcome.

What they really need to do, then, is pitch their view as the babyface, and their opponent's view as the heel, and show why the reader should root for the babyface, and how the babyface can ultimately overcome the heel. Here is how we might do this in analogy with Snow's steps above:

Philosophy's "Seven Deadly Steps":

1. Shine the author's proposal, and mention the benefits the view would bring.
2. The Heat Spot – discuss serious problems raised for the view.
3. Heel Beatdown – highlight the significance of the problems and how others have failed to solve them.
4. The Hope Spot – give new response to problems.
5. The Double Down – show the new response still leaves significant questions unanswered. What can possibly be done?

6. The Comeback – describe alternative way of thinking about new response which answers these questions.
7. The Finish – show how the author's view emerges victorious.

This sort of narrative structure is not at all uncommon in the construction of philosophical works, and the method used is designed for very similar purposes to the method used to construct pro wrestling matches: to elicit a particular response from the audience (in this case, the reader), and to make the reader root for the author's view. If an author can do this, there is more chance that the reader will be persuaded by the author's argument, which is the main aim of the work in the first place.

Of course, I am not claiming that *all* philosophical works have this structure, just as Al Snow was not claiming that *all* pro wrestling matches have his structure, but it is a commonly used way of proceeding. Some papers do not have this structure at all, as they are not presenting views, just criticizing them. This is not to say that they don't have equivalents in pro wrestling match-forms, though. Primarily critical papers are more one-sided, and can have the feel of a pro wrestling squash match, where one wrestler (usually a heel) beats down their opponent whilst suffering very little damage. Other papers take the forms of "run-ins", where the author pitches the argument as an effort to defend another philosopher's view from an objection.

The general idea, then, is that the worked nature of a pro wrestling match does not detract from its similarities to a philosophical work. On the contrary, it makes it even more similar than it is to an amateur wrestling match. This is because, in philosophical works, arguments and debates are simulated or staged by the author as part of the case that they are making for their view. In Plato's dialogues, Plato simulates debate in order to establish the conclusions he wants to get to, and in many philosophical works one presents debates and arguments in such a way as to put one's own view in the best possible light.

Even if this idea holds for written philosophical work, what about "live action" philosophy found in public talks, presentations, and conferences?

3. Matches and Symposia

Pro wrestling typically combines elements of scripting and improvisation. Matches are scripted in that the winner of the match is determined in advance, usually by the booking committee, and the "finish" of the match is also decided, usually with the assistance of an agent designated to work with the wrestlers on the match. Sometimes the agent will help the wrestlers plan every move in the match in detail, and sometimes the wrestlers do this themselves (Macho Man Randy Savage was a wrestler who typically worked this way; see also the Ronda Rousey/Kurt Angle vs Stephanie McMahon/Triple H match from WrestleMania 34).

Other times wrestlers would "call it in the ring", in that they would improvise the specific moves in the match whilst having a general outline of how it would go (Ric Flair famously worked this way). Traditionally, in these circumstances, the heel would call the match, leading the babyface through the different phases. Improvising in this way requires a lot of skill: one needs to be attuned to the crowd, to have good knowledge of narrative structure, and the physical capability to think clearly and quickly during intense physical activity.

Philosophical events can also take on either scripted or improvised forms, sometimes with a mixture of the two. A symposium discussion, for example, is one where you have two or more philosophers presenting their views on a particular subject to an audience. The philosophers chosen usually have opposing, or at least different, views on the topic, and are expected to engage with one another, as well as the audience. They each get the chance to present their ideas, and courtesy is such that they share what they will say with each other before the event, so each knows what the other will say: it is bad form to deviate from this and spring unexpected surprises on the other person. There is an element of the unknown in that neither knows what the audience's responses and questions will be, but this is the equivalent of the element of the unknown that the crowd brings to a pro wrestling match: whilst the wrestlers know what each other will do, they do not know how the crowd will respond, and how they will need to react accordingly.

There is thus a significant degree of staging built into the norms and practices of philosophical discussion in person, as well as in print. The sorts of "combat" one sees in philosophical discussions more often than not will involve more pre-planned elements than unplanned elements, and exhibit many of the characteristics of the sorts of staging seen in pro wrestling matches. The uglier side of pro wrestling is also seen in philosophy, in part because of this hyper-masculine, combative atmosphere. Indeed, the historically combative nature of philosophical method both in print and in person is something lamented by many contemporary philosophers who aim to move philosophy away from this approach. Philosophy is a discipline overwhelmingly populated by white men, and conferences often present hostile environments to women, people of color, and LGBTQ philosophers. As a result, contemporary work on philosophical method by philosophers such as Janice Moulton (1983), Scott Aikin (2011), and Helen Beebee (2013) considers the "combative" model, and whether it is a good thing for philosophy. Just as pro wrestling has had to work on making a more inclusive environment, philosophy needs to too, and this may mean revisiting the fundamentals of the discipline.

Philosophy can take some other cues from the activity of pro wrestling here. As noted in chapter 6, a pro wrestler is not trying to *win* the match they're in; rather they're working collectively with their opponent in the service of a different cause: putting on a good match to entertain the audience. It takes two to tango, and wrestlers need to work together to achieve their goals. The same should apply in philosophy. Philosophy is not about winning arguments; rather, a philosophical discussion should be a collective enterprise where people work together to pursue the truth. If philosophers see themselves working together to achieve this goal, as opposed to each thinking that their goal is to beat the other in faux-combat to win the argument, then we get a better picture of what philosophy should be about, which may help create a more inclusive environment.

4. The Pro Wrestling of Philosophy

Considerations of the similarities between pro wrestling and philosophy lead us to some deep questions about the practice of philosophy, such as whether a philosopher believes the view or argument she puts forward, and whether she is required to do so. Pro wrestlers, for the most part, are "working" their audience, in the terms of the wrestling business: that is, they are pretending to fight, or pretending to dislike their opponents, as opposed to being engaged in a "shoot", where real feelings and real fights are involved. We can now ask the question of whether philosophy is a work or a shoot. Are philosophers "working" their audience by pretending to hold certain views to get their work published or noticed, or are they engaged in a "shoot" by writing things that they genuinely believe? Moreover, what should we expect of philosophers here? In increasingly competitive professional environments, is it too high an expectation that philosophers believe what they say, and, if so, what does this say about the value of sincerity in philosophical discourse?

5. What's Your Gimmick?

The aim of a pro wrestler is to get over with a crowd; to generate a reaction, either positive (for a babyface), or negative (for a heel). Having a good gimmick (character), and a good story, is a key part of this. A pro wrestler needs something distinctive to mark them out; to make them memorable. Likewise, a philosopher aims to "get over" with other philosophers, in that they want their work to be recognized and engaged with. The more over you are, the more your work is discussed; the more your work is cited, the more book contracts you get, and the more conference invitations you get. In order to get over, though, you need something distinctive about your work: you need a view; *a gimmick*. This can take a number of forms: it can be working on something that nobody else has worked on for a while, or it can be taking someone else's work and making minor amendments to it, or it can be founding a whole new view that nobody else has put forward, or it can be formulating and defending a view that everyone else thinks is crazy. The last option is the most impactful, though it is hard to pull off successfully. Perhaps the most famous example in contemporary philosophy is David Lewis's realism about possible worlds, which holds that every way a world could possibly be is the way some world is. All these worlds exist in the same "concrete" sense that our world does, though they are spatiotemporally sealed off from one another. A close second is David Benatar's "better never to have been" view that existence is a harm, and that everyone would have been better off if they had never existed.

These are great gimmicks: they are striking, shocking, and demand your attention as soon as you hear about them. They also got Lewis and Benatar more over as philosophers than they would otherwise have been, even if they were already over to a good degree before the views appeared. Not all gimmicks are like this; indeed, most are much more mundane, but having one is important.

Such is the value of having a good gimmick, and the question arises of whether philosophy is a work or a shoot: do philosophers believe the views they put forward, or are they working the audience; selling their gimmick?

6. Philosophy: Work or Shoot?

Imagine you're a philosophy grad student, starting to think about your doctoral dissertation. You know that the philosophy job market is incredibly competitive, and your chances of success are low. You talk to your advisor, and they emphasize the importance of originality: of having a view that makes you stand out; makes you memorable. So, you start to conduct your research with this in mind: what can I do that makes me stand out? Notice that doing things this way in no way requires that you end up with a view that you actually *believe*, just so long as it is something that is defensible, and stands out. (This is not to say that you don't believe in it as an idea, but this is not the same thing as actually believing what your view says.)

What's going on here is that you are directing your work with your audience in mind. You are constructing a project whose goal is to "pop" those reading about it. In wrestling talk, you are *working*. You are working in that you are putting on a show, playing a character, and stating views you do not have to believe. You are also working the audience, in that you are trying to capture the imagination of your readers to get them interested and engaged with your project.

Now let's suppose you get over. People are reading your work, discussing your work, inviting you to conferences, writing papers about your work. As your career progresses, you start to think more critically about your gimmick: it got you over, but do you really believe it? Does it matter? Maybe you do start to publicly question the view, and maybe you publicly denounce it, leaving others to take up the mantle. Or maybe you decide that the attention, the conferences, the edited volumes, are worth continuing to defend it, and continuing to associate your name with it. This decision is a decision about whether philosophy – to you – is a work or a shoot.

Some philosophers – most notably Ludwig Wittgenstein and Hilary Putnam – radically change their minds, and their views, throughout the course of their careers. They became known as "early Wittgenstein", "early Putnam", and "later Wittgenstein" and "later Putnam". This suggests a tone of academic integrity, in that they were willing to abandon views that made them famous in the pursuit of truth (though, more cynically, it is also a gimmick in itself, and another way to be noticed). These are rare exceptions though, and most philosophers stick to their main view through the course of their careers, albeit with amendments and clarifications made to the position. This may seem surprising, as why should we expect a philosopher aged 60 to still hold the same views they held when they are 30? One cynical answer is that if you make your name with a view, you are better positioned in the discipline if you stick to it, whatever your private doubts might be. Moreover, there is pressure to do so. If you are known for your views on a particular subject, when you're invited to give talks at conferences or other institutions, usually they will want you to talk about that: that's why you were invited, after all. If you show up and talk about something completely different, or start trashing your own views, you're not really doing what's expected of you as an invited speaker.

This is not to say that there's anything wrong with *working* as a philosopher. Being an academic is a job after all, the thing that is one's work, and part of that job is coming up with and defending views. If one sees one's work as merely one's job, then working makes sense. I guess the issue is, though, whether we see philosophy – as a subject – as something worthy of nobler intentions. If philosophers are just working and trying to get over, then the subject itself becomes rather meaning-less. A view may not advance our understanding of something, or get us closer to the truth about a topic, if all it is intended to do is get its proponent over. Indeed, it may run contrary to this purpose.

Interestingly, this takes us back to Ancient Greece, and Protagoras, who (as we noted earlier) called his book on truth *The Throws*. Protagoras is often described as a "Sophist", or "wise person", in contrast to someone like Socrates, who is described as a "philosopher", or "lover of wisdom". The Sophists as a group of thinkers get a pretty bad rap in the history of philosophy. The distinctive claim of the Sophists is "to make the weaker argument the stronger". The Sophists were teachers, who sold the development of skills in argumentation to young Athenians looking to make their way in the world. Students were taught how to argue effectively for a position, and – crucially – there was no requirement that they actually believe the view that they were arguing for. All that mattered was that they could argue effec-tively. The Sophists were viewed by people like Socrates and Plato as a great threat to the good name of philosophy, as they employed similar methods to philosophers – arguments – but in ways that could be a lot more directed toward personal gain and advancement than arguments were intended to be in philosophy: the difference between a Sophist and a philosopher is that a philosopher cares for the truth, whereas the Sophist cares about winning the argument. Indeed, it wasn't just philosophers who had a problem with the Sophists, but, eventually, Athenian society in general, and one of the reasons Socrates was ultimately executed was because he was widely perceived to be a Sophist.

If what's been said above is correct, it is not a stretch to say that philosophy as it is practiced today could be accused of sophistry. As we've already talked about, what's prized is having a distinctive view, that you can argue for well, that gets noticed. This requires a great deal of creativity and argumentative skill, but it does not in addition require a concern for the truth. The skills that philosophers teach undergraduates and graduate students are largely critical thinking skills, skills that enable one to effectively criticize and construct arguments. To retain an important element of *philosophy*, we need to remember that philosophy is ultimately about pursuing truth, not trying to sound clever or sophisticated.

What should the upshot of this be, then? Should philosophers really believe the views they put forward? Should philosophy always be a shoot, and never a work? This seems too strict a constraint, but philosophers should be mindful of the potential harm that working their audience can do to the legitimacy of the subject as a whole. If, as argued in this book, thinking about pro wrestling can make us philosophers, philosophers also have to be mindful of the things that make them philosophers, and not be too tempted by the glitz and glamour of a good gimmick: that is one thing that should be left to pro wrestling!

Lastly, as I hope this book has made clear, philosophy is not just something for the academy, confined to academics in colleges and universities. In this case, we can do philosophy by thinking about pro wrestling, and it can be done by anybody who wants to spend a bit of time thinking and discussing key issues. In fact, a lot of pro wrestling fans are already doing philosophy without even knowing it. Philosophy, in many respects, has a mainstream image problem just as significant – if not more so – than pro wrestling does, in that it is often marginalized and frequently misunderstood. To change this, we need to show how philosophy happens all around us, and in places we might not expect. Philosophy should be accessible and intelligible to anyone, not locked away in ivory towers. And that's the bottom line, 'cause this philosopher said so!

Credits

I hope you've had as much fun reading this book as I did writing it. I hope too that you see the worth of thinking about pro wrestling and philosophy together, even if you don't agree with everything I've said. In fact, it's good if you don't agree with me about everything, as philosophy is about discussion, and what I want this book to do, above all else, is to prompt enjoyable thought and debate. There's also a lot more to say about all the things discussed here, and many more issues to consider. I haven't tried to cover everything, and this is hopefully just the beginning of the pro wrestling–philosophy tag team that could go on to win many titles.

Full references are given below for sources mentioned in the text. I also wanted to acknowledge the number of influences from various sources that have informed my understanding of pro wrestling over the years. I have read many books, watched many hours of TV, and listened to countless hours of podcasts, and thoroughly enjoyed every minute of it. Despite all this time spent, there is so much amazing stuff out there that I haven't been able to get to, and my apologies if you think I have missed something important – I will get to it soon!

1. Wrestling Shows Discussed

For WWF, WWE, NXT, WCW and ECW shows, *WWE Network*: http://www.wwe.com/network

For New Japan Pro Wrestling shows, *New Japan World*: https://njpw world.com

AEW, *Being the Elite*: https://www.youtube.com/beingtheelite

AEW YouTube Channel: https://www.youtube.com/allelitewrestling

Ring of Honor: https://www.rohwrestling.com

Beyond Wrestling: https://www.youtube.com/user/BeyondWrestling

Quintessential Pro Wrestling: playlist at youtube.com

2. Wrestling Podcasts

The Steve Austin Show by Steve Austin. The Al Snow episode was on *The Steve Austin Show – Unleashed!,* released on January 4, 2018.

Talk is Jericho by Chris Jericho. The Jon Moxley episode was released on May 29, 2019.

Something to Wrestle with Bruce Prichard by Bruce Prichard and Conrad Thompson

What Happened When with Tony Schiavone by Tony Schiavone and Conrad Thompson

83 Weeks with Eric Bischoff by Eric Bischoff and Conrad Thompson

The Jim Cornette Experience by Jim Cornette

E & C's Pod of Awesomeness by Adam "Edge" Copeland and Jay "Christian" Reso

The Lawcast by Cewsh and the Law

We Enjoy Wrestling by Matt Fowler, Eric Goldman and April Johnson

The WrestleRamble Podcast by Luke Owen, Oli Davis et al.

"The Montreal Screwjob", *RadioLab*, Jad Abumrad and Robert Krulwich, February 24, 2015

WrestlingInc WINCLY, March 12, 2019

3. Wrestling News Websites

The Wrestling Observer at f4wonline.com (The match length statistics for the WrestleMania 35 matches mentioned in chapter 2 were from the April 15 edition, with thanks also to Wrestling With Stats, @GrapsWithStats.)

Pro Wrestling Torch at pwtorch.com

Rajah.com

Fightful.com

WrestleTalk.com

Cagesideseats.com

WrestlingInc.com

WrestleCrap.com

Belltobelles.com

4. Wrestling Documentaries/TV Shows

Hitman Hart: Wrestling with Shadows, Paul Jay, 1998

Beyond the Mat, Barry Blaustein, 1999

André the Giant, Jason Hehir, HBO, 2018

Nature Boy, ESPN 30 for 30, Rory Karph, ESPN, 2017

Dark Side of the Ring: The Match Made in Heaven, Viceland, 2019

Dark Side of the Ring: The Montreal Screwjob, Viceland, 2019

Why the News Media is Stealing from the Pro Wrestling Playbook, Tedx Naperville Talk, Eric Bischoff, November 30, 2018

Last Week Tonight with John Oliver, HBO, March 31, 2019

The Rise of the Attitude Era, Jim Ross and Jim Cornette, WhatCulture
  Inside the Ropes LIVE Q&A, April 28, 2017

Total Divas, E! & WWE Network, 2013–

Total Bellas, E! & WWE Network, 2016–

Miz and Mrs, USA Network, 2018–

WWE Confidential, WWE Network, 2002–3

5. Books about Wrestling

Scott M. Beekman, *Ringside: A History of Professional Wrestling in
  America*, Praeger Publishers, 2006

Eric Bischoff (with Jeremy Roberts), *Controversy Creates Cash*, WWE
  & Pocket Books, 2006

James Dixon and Justin Henry, *Titan Screwed: Lost Smiles, Stunners,
  and Screwjobs*, WhatCulture.com, 2016

Guy Evans, *Nitro: The Incredible Rise and Inevitable Collapse of Ted
  Turner's WCW*, 2018

Mick Foley, *Mankind: Have a Nice Day*, WWE & HarperCollins,
  1999

Mick Foley, *Foley is Good: And the Real World is* Faker *than Wrestling*,
  WWE & HarperCollins, 2001

Mick Foley, *The Hardcore Diaries*, WWE & Pocket Books, 2006

Marcus Griffin, *Fall Guys: The Barnums of Bounce*, The Reilly and Lee
  Co., 1937

Bret Hart, *Hitman: My Real Life in the Cartoon World of Wrestling*,
  Random House, 2007

Chris Jericho, *A Lion's Tale: Around the World in Spandex*, Grand
  Central Publishing, 2007

Chris Jericho, *Undisputed: How to Become the World Champion in 1,372 Easy Steps*, Grand Central Publishing, 2011

Chris Jericho, *The Best in the World: At What I Have No Idea*, Gotham Books, 2014

Heather Levi, *The World of Lucha Libre: Secrets, Revelations, and Mexican National Identity*, Duke University Press, 2008

Sean Oliver, *Kayfabe: Stories You're Not Supposed to Hear from a Pro Wrestling Production Company Owner*, CreateSpace, 2017.

Nicholas Sammond (ed.), *Steel Chair to the Head: The Pleasure and Pain of Professional Wrestling*, Duke University Press, 2005

6. Articles Referred To

Roland Barthes, "The World of Wrestling", in his *Mythologies*, Hill and Wang, 1972

Ted Butryn, "Global Smackdown: Vince McMahon, World Wrestling Entertainment, and Neoliberalism", in D. Andrews and M. Silk (eds.) *Sport and Neoliberalism: Politics, Consumption, and Culture*, Temple University Press, 2012

Jeffrey Jerome Cohen, "Monster Culture (seven theses)", in Jeffrey Cohen (ed.), *Monster Theory: Reading Culture*, University of Minnesota Press, 1996

Hallie Grossman, "Equal Fights Movement", http://www.espn.com/espnw/feature/24364018/intergender-wrestling-equality-wo men-violence-them

Graham Isador, "LGBTQ Pro Wrestlers Say There's Never Been a Better Time to Be Queer in the Ring", https://www.vice.com/en_ca/article/paj4dn/lgbtq-pro-wrestlers-say-theres-never-been-a-better-time-to-be-queer-in-the-ring

Henry Jenkins III, "Afterword, Part 1: Wrestling with Theory, Grappling with Politics", in Nicholas Sammond (ed.), *Steel Chair to the Head: The Pleasure and Pain of Professional Wrestling*, Duke University Press, 2005

Lia Miller, "To Wrestling Offense, a Cultural Defense", *New York Times*, July 18, 2005

Rachel, "that one tweet thread about the Golden Lovers, annotated", https://medium.com/we-need-to-talk-about-wrestling/that-one-tweet-thread-about-the-golden-lovers-annotated-e9fc604e3a7f

Mairead Small Staid, "Does WWE Really Want a Revolution?", https://www.theringer.com/2018/10/25/18022514/wwe-evolution-revolution-womens-wrestling-shimmer

Oscar Wilde, "The Decay of Lying", in his *Intentions*, 1891. Available at https://www.gutenberg.org/ebooks/887

WrestlingInc.com, interview with Muhammad Hassan: https://www.wrestlinginc.com/news/2016/02/muhammad-hassan-first-full-interview-in-years-heat-in-wwe-607505/

7. Philosophy Works Referred To

Scott Aikin, "A Defense of War and Sport Metaphors in Argument", *Philosophy & Rhetoric*, 44:3 (2011), 250–72

Aristotle, *Nicomachean Ethics*, trans. J.A.K. Thomson, Penguin Classics, 1955

Helen Beebee, "Women and Deviance in Philosophy", in K. Hutchison and F. Jenkins (eds.), *Women in Philosophy: What Needs to Change?* Oxford University Press, 2013

David Benatar, *Better Never to Have Been: The Harm of Coming into Existence*, Oxford University Press, 2016

Judith Butler, "Performative Acts and Gender Constitution: An Essay in Phenomenology and Feminist Theory", *Theatre Journal*, 40:4 (1988), 519–31

Epictetus, *Handbook*, trans. E. Carter, available at: http://classics.mit.edu/Epictetus/epicench.html

Allen Guttmann, *From Ritual to Record: The Nature of Modern Sports*, Columbia University Press, 1978

David Hume, *A Treatise of Human Nature*, 1738, available at early-moderntexts.com

Lisa Jones, "All Caught Up in the Kayfabe: Understanding and Appreciating Pro-Wrestling", *Journal of the Philosophy of Sport*, 46:2 (2019), 276–91

David Lewis, *A Plurality of Worlds*, Blackwell, 1986

Janice Moulton, "A Paradigm of Philosophy: The Adversary Method", in S. Harding and M.N. Hintikka (eds.), *Discovering Reality: Feminist Perspectives on Epistemology, Metaphysics, Methodology, and Philosophy of Science*, Kluwer Academic Publishers, 1983

Derek Parfit, *Reasons and Persons*, Oxford University Press, 1984

Plato, *The Republic*, trans. B. Jowett, available at: http://classics.mit.edu/Plato/republic.html

Plato, *Phaedo*, trans. B. Jowett, available at: http://classics.mit.edu/Plato/phaedo.html

Plato, *Euthyphro*, trans. B. Jowett, available at: http://classics.mit.edu/Plato/euthyfro.html

Bernard Suits, "Tricky Triad: Games, Play, and Sport", *Journal of the Philosophy of Sport*, 15:1 (1988), 1–9

Kendall Walton, "'It's Only a Game!': Sports as Fiction", in his *In Other Shoes: Music, Metaphor, Empathy, Existence*, Oxford University Press, 2015

Ludwig Wittgenstein, *Philosophical Investigations*, Blackwell, 1953

8. My Other Books

In case you're interested in my other philosophy books, they all address topics discussed here, including – particularly – truth and reality.

The Metaphysics of Truth (Oxford University Press, 2018) is a research monograph setting out my pluralist approach to truth. This book was awarded the 2019 Sanders Book Prize by the American Philosophical Association, which is awarded to the best book in philosophy of mind, metaphysics, or epistemology that engages the analytic tradition published in English in the previous five-year period.

Properties (Polity Press, 2014) is an introductory book on the nature of properties.

Truth: A Contemporary Reader (Bloomsbury Press, 2019) is a collection I edited introducing the main approaches to the nature and value of truth.

Index of Names